Putting a Different Spin on It

Coaching Cricket from an Alternative Perspective

By Peter Wright

Putting a Different Spin on It

Coaching Cricket from an Alternative Perspective

Sports Education and Performance Development

© Peter Wright 2017
ISBN – 978-0-244-61062-3

All rights reserved. No part of this publication may be reproduced, stored in or introduced into a retrieval system, or transmitted, in any form, or by any means (electronic, mechanical, photocopying, recording, or otherwise) without the prior written permission of the author or publisher.

"You've got to be very careful if you don't know where you're going, because you might not get there."

~ Yogi Berra

Table of Contents

Foreword by Louise Deeley, CPsychol, AFBPsS 9
Dedications 13
Introduction 17
Philosophy 21
Becoming the Maverick...27
The Maverick's Toolkit...33
The Casebook...39
    Keeping it "Simples" 41
    Remember to Breathe 47
    The Silence of the Ticking Clock........................49
    Where do you think you're going?.....................59
    The Book of Judgement..65
    Confidence and the Leap of Faith.......................71
    Impersonal 77
    Do 8 year olds think outside the box?................87
    Decision Making 91
    Working outside the Bubble of Expertise.........97
    Suck it and See..101
    Under the Radar...105
    Can you put it in a Wheelbarrow 113

What Happens when you do X? 117
Reframing the Critical Voice 121
Keep Your Conscious Clear......................125
The Clasped Fingers Trick........................129
The Power of Now 133
Weaving Spells with Localised Trance 139
Piling Everything onto The Learning Curve.........147
Watch Your Own Performance..............159
The Session Built on Magic......................165
Work in Progress..173
When to ease the Cognitive Load..........177
A Partridge in a Petrie..............................187
Culture Shock 193
Attention Awareness Focus and Concentration...199
Resilience...207
Our Stance in Life......................................217
Learning from Mr. Li................................223

Footnotes 231
Recommended Reading 233
About the Author...235

Foreword by Louise Deeley, CPsychol, AFBPsS

I first had the pleasure of meeting Peter at a one day 'Introduction to NLP for Sport' workshop I presented for the British Association of Sport and Exercises Sciences, back in March 2007, and clearly it was a 'meeting of two *maverick* minds'!

Anyone reading this who is familiar with the concept of introducing anything *slightly* left field into scientific circles will understand the resistance some academics *used* to hold about NLP, (and sadly, *some* still do!). And despite its track record in business, and me being a senior lecturer in Sport Psychology, a Sport Scientist and a BPS Sport Psychologist, there was much scepticism and 'rumblings' about the validity of NLP as a 'science' at this workshop.

But not Peter.

Peter was lit up like a beacon, excited and enthused by the practical opportunities NLP could offer. As an experienced hypnotherapist already, Peter realised that it wasn't about the 'scientific research' per se, but more about the practical application and opportunities that

NLP, combined with hypnosis *and* his experiences as a sports coach could bring to the many athletes and sports enthusiasts that he worked alongside to help them grow and develop.

Talk about a breath of fresh air!

Not only did I have my confidence reassured about the usefulness of NLP to the sport practitioner, but I had met someone who was open-minded, passionate about his 'athlete charges' and recognised the importance of looking beyond the status quo.

That initial meeting led into a 10 year friendship, where clearly the importance of doing things differently and paying attention to what *really* works, rather than what we're told is the *correct* way, is something important to us both.

So, not quite exactly 10 years on, (give or take a few days!), I find myself writing this foreword with a big smile on my face, as I reflect on the way the world works.

You see, Peter and I met up in November 2016, to 'chew the fat', talk about shared experiences of using NLP in sport ... specifically in cricket which is a passion for both of us *and* have an excuse for expensive coffees ... and of course what was coming up next?

Because of Peter's unique eye for 'the difference' and his long-term passion for writing about *Coaching Cricket from an Alternative Perspective*, I flippantly said, 'you should gather your written musings into a book and call it "Putting a different spin on it"!

The rest you can say is history, as this book is exactly what Peter has done!

Reading through it I know I won't be the only one it delights and engages, and Peter's many reflections, commentaries and ideas are written in a way that not only makes sense on many levels but makes you want to keep reading right the way through to the end.

The casebook approach offers the reader bite-sized insights and reflections that are all the better for NOT giving you 'the answer'. Rather, they conversationally describe situations, offer consideration and insight and allow you to draw conclusions, relate to your own experiences and ultimately start to unravel ways in which you might approach and formulate solutions to the vagaries that working with human beings and sport offers.

For those of you familiar with NLP, you'll recognise the many ways this is implicitly inter-woven into the casebook commentaries, and even if you've never even heard of it, there is much that this book offers around the *thinking about* the art of coaching, alternative philosophies, and possibly most importantly, the human way in which Peter approaches what clearly is a lifelong love and passion that he imparts to everyone lucky enough to cross his path.

I loved this collection, it's warm, it's engaging and it's thought provoking and you will smile and nod with recognition of the situations described that don't fall within the coaching manual, and have left you wondering 'now how do I deal with this'!

I *should* say 'if you're serious about your coaching, you should read this collection', but what I *will* say is, 'if you want to think, feel and approach your coaching *without* boundaries, feeling stumped or being caught behind, then you DEFINITELY should read this book.

Dedications

Standing on the shoulders of Giants

Whatever we achieve in life, whatever we set out to do, there is always a handful of very special people who we have looked up to in our formative years, who have built the fire under our passion, and set it alight with theirs.

In terms of my cricket and my coaching I have three such giants, and without them I would never ever have trod this amazing pathway.

The first was my Uncle Tom. He was a Yorkshireman and a *"Dalesman"* – imbued with the Yorkshire spirit that said, "Thou shalt love Cricket!" Now, I was born in Yorkshire, so I could, at some future point, perhaps play cricket for Yorkshire. Though they have since been changed, those were the qualifying rules for Yorkshire cricket back when I was young. My Uncle took responsibility for ensuring that I would play AND love cricket – and I think now, looking down from above, he'd be rather pleased with his handiwork!

The second was the man who, single-handedly, inspired me to become a coach. His name was Rodney Beer, head of sport at Ilfracombe Grammar School in Devon. Now I wasn't a pupil of Rodney's, but my school played cricket and rugby against Ilfracombe Grammar and we all knew about his somewhat legendary status as a games master!

As I left school and my life developed and unfolded, I soon found myself playing rugby at Ilfracombe RFC – where Rodney was Chairman. This was where his influence upon me as a thinker and player of sport really began to flourish. To say he was an inspiration was something of an understatement. He coached and trained us on a weekly basis, at a time – in the 1970s – when grass roots rugby players NEVER trained, let alone were coached! He imbued in us all a sense of striving for continuous individual improvement and excellence in team performance. We would, quite literally, have all jumped off a cliff for him – if he were to ask.

I was very grateful that, many years later when I was coaching at the same Club, I had the chance to thank him for his influence and inspiration, and how he had been instrumental in changing both my sporting outlook and, indeed, my life.

The third giant was former Somerset CCC opening batsman, Brian Roe. Brian did not only have an exceptional cricketing brain, but he also had an almost flawless batting technique, and an accuracy as a bowler that seemed to defy all odds.
In his later years, after his retirement from playing for Somerset, I was exceptionally fortunate to have been a playing and club colleague of Brian's.

Brian wasn't a coach, and he wasn't a player either – he was a Master in every sense. Along with the rest of my team mates, I learned huge amount about the game from just observing him and listening to his insightful comments. Every game shared was not just a joy, but also a learning opportunity.
Even now, if a player asks me about some part of their technique, my first thought – before even answering – would be, "How would Brian answer this one?"

When batting, he had so much time and composure it was unreal. He would call exactly the right amount of runs for every shot he played, regardless of the fielders or the state of the ground. He would pace his running in such a manner that he would make his ground just a split second before the throw arrived.
He also had a canny understanding of the psyche of his

opponents, garnered no doubt from years of experience in the 1st Class game.

Brian was, without doubt, the greatest influence on my cricket as a player and as a coach – and still is now.

When I work at what I love, there is nothing more rewarding than to see players flourish and enjoy a love of the game similar to my own – a love, and a passion, handed down to me from the hands of my Giants.

Introduction

I have played the game of cricket for over 60 years. It has been a huge part of my life, and has also helped me to understand Life in ways that only a continued experience and a Love of the Game can bring.

My cricket began with family members, on the beach, with a wooden bat and a rubber ball. When I was 8 or 9, and lived in what is now Malawi, in central Africa, I played with a group of schoolmates in one of their gardens. We had a proper hard cricket ball, a proper adult sized bat and two sets of stumps and bails and that was it. We had no gloves, or pads, or boxes – and this was long before the days of helmets.
During days of what seemed like endless sunshine, we would play cricket for hours after school and at weekends. We taught ourselves how to bat, bowl and field. It was simple – yet also **hard school** compared to today. We all suffered plenty of bruised fingers and shins, yet we all learned that the bat, together with our sharp wits, were our only means of protection! And, interestingly, no one ever got hit in the face either! I must have been 16 and back at school in England before I ever encountered a proper Cricket coach!

In terms of my own coaching journey, Cricket wasn't the first sport I coached – that was Skiing in 1977, which I coached some nine months after a knee injury in Rugby. At the time of the injury I thought it would affect my mobility for the rest of my life - and certainly that it would be the end of ALL my active sporting days. Fortunately for me it turned out not to be so, and I discovered I was still able to Ski and so subsequently started to play Cricket once more.

I began coaching Cricket formally in 1992, yet at the start of that time I merely tutored young players in the technicalities that I understood of, and with the love and the passion that I had for, the Game. It was a good place to start, and is probably the way that most players set out to *"pass the game on to the next generation"* by inviting them to **"model me"**.

Over the last 25 years I must have coached many thousands of players of varying ages. Some of them have been adult players, yet most of those I've been privileged to coach have been children – the youngest of which was aged 4!

Along the way, I've coached players at County level - who have since gone on to become professional players in the 1st Class game – right down to working with children in Reception Classes at schools.

Just playing the game – and still being able to play it – is a love, for me. Coaching the game, however, is a *passion* that keeps me fit, active, motivated and exceedingly young at heart. I still coach cricket at Clubs and schools and in the summer of 2017 some weeks I spent upwards of 30 hours a week both coaching and playing the game.

I'm exceptionally fortunate in that I'm still able to work at something I love doing and - being decidedly *left field* in my approach to Life and Sport - I have been able to experience some very interesting and off-the-wall happenings in the course of my coaching.

As a prolific writer of books and articles, I have been encouraged and persuaded by colleagues and friends to bring together and publish some of these anecdotes, discoveries and observations.

So, this is my collected *Casebook* of some of those off-the-wall encounters along the less-travelled road of Coaching Cricket from an Alternative Perspective.

Philosophy

All life and, in the particular of life, all sport - begins with Love. Rather like Life, Sport is about play. And yet there are many, many people who treat life AND their sport as anything but Play – which rather begs the question ...
WHERE, then, IS THE LOVE?

My first tenet in the philosophy of sport is that you have to love it. That way you will keep coming back to it – unless, perish the thought, you happen to fall out of Love with it. However, when any "falling out of love" happens – then it is usually down to something other than Love.
Remember – ***Love Conquers All*** – so if you love your sport, and there's a lot of not so good stuff going on in the rest of your life, then GO PLAY. And you'll find that once you immerse yourself **fully** into THAT love, then it will conquer all, in the moments that you are engaged with it.

So, I start with Love – and the next tenet is the one I have already mentioned – PLAY.

There's a great book by Stuart Brown called *"Play: How it Shapes the Brain, Opens the Imagination, and Invigorates the Soul."* It is a book I would recommend to all coaches, of whatever persuasion - Sport or otherwise. It sorts out the simple, directional stuff and answers the "Why do we do it?" question.

Now a lot of Sport involves dedicated practice – which is where, most often in practical terms, COACH MEETS PLAYER.

In my interaction with clients and players, there are three main areas I work in –

Educating, Conditioning and Performance.

Yet, when it comes to my Coaching Philosophy in these three areas - here's the thing...

Players, clients (call them what you will) ALL have to buy in to LOVE and PLAY. When they do, ALL learning, conditioning and performing becomes not only FUN, but also VERY MUCH EASIER.
We, as humans, gravitate towards things we like doing and, along the way, we discover we get GOOD at those things much more quickly than the things we don't like doing.

In our early years we have a curiosity about everything AND, consequently, we get to learn everything quickly. Now somewhere along the way, between the ages of 5 and 7, the simplicities of Living and Learning and Getting Good – LIKE THAT – seem to become complicated.

And it's not that the **things** become complicated you understand, but it's that our attitude gets more complex.

And thus it is, when we complicate our attitudes, how everything then gets much harder.

There's a great quote pertaining to any one of the aforementioned trio of *Educating, Conditioning and Performance*, in Robert M Pirsig's book *Zen and the Art of Motorcycle Maintenance* ~

"Is it hard?'
Not if you have the right attitudes. Its having the right attitudes that's hard."

My philosophical approach to Performance AND Practice therefore is to keep Love, Play and Fun at the top of the agenda.

"Education is the kindling of a flame, not the filling of a vessel" ~   Socrates

"When the only tool in your toolkit is a hammer then you tend to see every problem as a nail"   ~   Abraham Maslow

"Stop thinking and end your problems"
                             ~   Lao Tzu

"We keep moving forward, opening new doors, and doing new things, because we're curious and curiosity keeps leading us down new paths"   ~   Walt Disney

These four particular quotes have had considerable influence upon me over the years. I could even say that they are the grounded pillars upon which my coaching perspective has been placed.

Socrates tells us the true nature of how we might best learn about ***anything***, at any time in our entire lives. The kindling of a flame implies ***Passion*** – and for me the presence of passion gives learning a purpose. When I went to school, Education was far less of a system than it is now – indeed we still had the idea of it being the kindling of a flame. *Ergo,* part of why I enjoy writing and find it comes easy to me, was the flame kindled by my English teacher at secondary school.

Maslow's quote pointed me towards discovering things or actions that produced results that WORKED BETTER than the generally accepted ones. The entire Hypnotic and Neuro-Linguistic Domains were a particular case in point for me, for suddenly I was acquiring a wonderful set of tools to add to the hammer in my toolkit. Now, I realised that I could help people with elegance and efficiency – and not repeatedly bludgeon them with that "trusty" hammer!

Lao Tzu's quote tells me about the true nature of our relationship with the Power of Thought. All our problems boil down to this one essential source – we all have a tendency to believe our thinking in the moment.

Walt Disney has an extraordinary ability to understand AND depict Mankind's innate curiosity through the power of story, characters, myth and fable. This keeps us all "childlike" and Young at Heart.

Becoming the Maverick

In truth I started out as an ordinary, conventional coach. I consulted the conventional "How To" manuals, modelled "How To" coaches as they delivered conventional "How To" sessions, and arrived at conclusions that led me to *"believe in the believables"*. And the greatest of all the believables is the one that avers, **"THIS is how it works."**

The next believable is the one that answers the question, "What happens when it doesn't work – or the player(s) I'm coaching don't get it?" And that answer is, **"YOU can't be doing it right.** Try again, go back and study your manuals, re-model other coaches, and bring yourself more into line with *"THIS is how it works."* Then it WILL work!

Now sometimes there IS ONLY convention when it comes to Coaching. Yet, the principles should NOT be set in stone for, in coaching, we are dealing with PEOPLE not ROBOTS. And people are notoriously diverse, fickle, awkward, individualistic and unpredictable.

It was here, amidst the endlessness of humanity's grey-scaling, that I stepped out of the conventional mainstream. To paraphrase the song *"Proud"* - I stepped out of the ordinary, and ascended into something that I have always found to be utterly EXTRA-ordinary.

The Human Mind

It happened one day when I was coaching a group of young cricketers. A fellow coach was observing me as I explained some elements of what we were going to be doing next - and when I'd finished, and whilst the players went off to get themselves ready, he asked me, *"Did you notice the kids' faces and how they paid attention?"*
"No," I replied, shaking my head.
"They were hanging off your every word. You could have quoted the phone book to them and they would still have been captivated."
"Blimey!" I said. "I wasn't aware of that!"

I realised then that it wasn't so much about **what** I was coaching (the content) rather it was **the way** I was communicating with the children, that was holding their rather spellbound attention. I figured it was this

that was enabling the players to learn quicker and more fully, and thus become better players.
It was very clear to me that for this to be happening then at some point there had to be a
Meeting of Minds.

I then remembered instances from my schooldays and formal education; I remembered events from my own sporting, stage, musical and other performances both social and personal; and I ran these past this whole idea of the *Meeting of Minds* and they all now made complete sense. From that moment I understood that **The Mind** is the crucial key to each and every Performance.

Round about this time I read the following passage from the *Preface* to *The Inner Game of Golf* by Tim Gallwey:-

"If human beings did not have the tendency to interfere with their own ability to perform and learn, there would be no Inner Game..... But the fact is that because of self-interference, few of us perform up to the level of our potential for more than brief

moments at a time. Learning to get out of one's way is the purpose of the Inner Game."

This was the ultimate reassurance that I was on the right track. The Inner Game is the vital key. It is what draws all the outer elements together. Without it we are reduced to mere robots – with it we can be elevated to whatever level WE choose. We just need to get out of our own way!

For me it was farewell to Conventional as I now was fully immersed, and fully committed, to being Maverick.

Ability and Capability

All languages are full of their own little linguistic "tricks" and ambiguities. English is no exception.

We ALL have abilities. They are innate, in our nature, and we are born with them – albeit in a very raw state. We then grow our abilities – starting with how we move and manipulate our bodies, and how we communicate.

Then – at some point in our youth – we begin to CAP most of our abilities. We CAP, or limit our abilities through believing we are just plain ordinary.

Some people break out of that illusion and AMAZE us. We MARVEL at their abilities, their dedication, and their sacrifices.
But WE could never be like that – because even though we were born uniquely extraordinary and believed in that truth for a while, the "Grown Up" World (and how it works) conspired to repeatedly tell us all about the things that we CAN'T do, not what we CAN.

Sadly most of us, before we have even reached the age of 10, have already garnered enough CAPS, enough limitations on our abilities, to last us for the rest of our lives. Equally sadly, most of us hold onto the beliefs about what we are and are not capable of – and live out our lives accordingly.

The World of the Maverick Coach says "HOLD ON!" "There is cap, NO ceiling on your possibilities and abilities. THERE is only the matter of HOW and WHEN."

And that Maverick Coach worldview goes on,
"I believe in you, but you have to believe in yourself. I can point you there, but *you* have to have the curiosity and passion to get there."

The Maverick's Toolkit

"Excellence in Sport has no beginning and no end; it IS merely about developing. No one can ever know it all, yet we can always progress. There is no such thing as the ultimate victory; everything is just a step along the way."

Quite early in my "journey" I came up with this quote. I've never seen anything similar elsewhere and concluded that it just came to me *out of the blue* – as a piece of wisdom! I also saw that I could exchange the word *Sport* for *Life* and it rang even more loud and clear! What I didn't perceive, at the time of course, was that I was assembling my "Maverick's Toolkit".

This was the understanding of how to enrich my various languages of communication; how to understand what makes people "tick"; how to see and carry out solutions to people's problems that seem insoluble; how to hold the "guiding torch" so that players could see their way clear.

The "Maverick's Toolkit" is a succession of how-to's that work. And here's the thing:-

Once you become a Maverick, and discover that that Toolkit just grows and grows, you come to understand that the entire universe is full of endless possibilities. And, it is here, I believe, where all Mavericks – in whatever field – GET IT.
"Get what?"
You may well ask – so I'll explain!

Our Relationship with our Thinking

Our entire lives are predicated on how we think "The World" works. What lies behind that driving force, that predication? What we know and understand is REAL! However, what You and I and We and They think is REAL is never entirely the same – WHY is that?

Because we ALL have slightly different perspectives.

Now I might agree with YOU about some things, but not EVERY thing, and *vice versa*. And here is the beginning of how both YOU and I might CHANGE

OUR MINDS about some things through our influence upon each other. NOW, suddenly or over a period of time – our perspectives have changed, and we see things differently.
And when we change our MINDS and see things differently, we change our perspectives.

What was once REAL in our perspectives is no longer REAL – but has now been replaced by a new REAL.
This rather begs the question –
"Was it EVER really real in the first place?"
And the answer is – NO!
We only THOUGHT it was real!
We believed our THINKING .

The Relationship with our Thinking shapes our Perceptions, our Judgements and Decisions, our Behaviour, and our Learning, Conditioning and Performance

For me, as a Maverick Coach, the moment we understand that what we think is merely an ILLUSION, then the World truly does become a series of endless possibilities.

Understanding That Relationship

Our understanding grows from knowing and discovering more about what can influence our Relationship with our Thinking.

- The nature of Temperament.
- The importance of and the effects of Language - both verbal and non-verbal.
- The nature of Awareness – of what is Conscious and Unconscious.

We can drill down into these influences and encounter further detailed understanding such as:-

- How breathing affects Temperament
- How Temperament affects States of Mind
- How a single Thought can grow into an Idea and eventually into a Belief, and how beliefs, attitudes and mindsets all affect our Perceptions, Decisions, Behaviours and Performance.
- How Language and Inner Dialogue (our talk to ourselves) can influence the level of our Consciousness and Temperament, States of Mind and consequently Perceptions, Decisions, Behaviours and Performance.

- How Awareness can be directed in both a Conscious and Unconscious way, and how the nature of Awareness influences the ability to Concentrate.
- The Nature of Concentration, its constituent parts of Attention and Focus and the variety of ways we can direct it.
- The Nature of Hypnotic Phenomena within both Unconscious and Conscious Awareness, and how they influence Perceptions, Decisions, Behaviour and Performance.

There's a crucial thing to know about the *Power of Thought* which is this:-

The *Power of Thought* flows through the entirety of our waking Consciousness. It is not OURS at this stage – it just IS. What we IGNORE just flows on – it does not become part of our thinking. What we NOTICE, or pay attention to, becomes OURS, becomes part of our thinking. And once it has become OURS the RELATIONSHIP begins.

Within the ensuing *Casebook* there are a variety of anecdotes concerning my coaching influence upon players of all ages.

All of these relate to topics I have mentioned that come under the umbrella of
"Our Relationship with Our Thinking."
Through reading them you will gain ideas and influences that will change your own views perhaps about your Cricket or your other sporting interests, and perhaps also about your Life in General. That is the way it is when ideas are shared – minds are opened – and perspectives are shifted.

At the foot of this page is the headline that forms part of my Blog. It contains lots of linguistic artifice. It is a rich English cake, full of flavour and device. Just for a bit of fun, see how much you can notice and identify!

"When we transform our thinking, our future presents us with something altogether more compelling!"

The Casebook

Keeping it "Simples"

It was the eve of the 2nd Cricket Test Match England v India 2011, and I was watching some televised interviews and film footage from the England Camp. I was just soaking up all the pre-match info, comment and banter when something involving Andrew Strauss, England Captain, that was going on in the filmed background, just seemed to catch my eye.

It set off a train of thought that came to rest around coaching - and not necessarily sports coaching - and how we all have ideas about what it is, what it entails, the preconceptions, misconceptions, methodologies and so on, and so forth.

Because of all this referencing - and the labelling that accompanies it - there is a something of a movement away from using *coaching*, as a concept, into other areas such as mentoring and training. Semantics and common parlance often force this change and movement, and for me - with connections in a number of paradigms - I feel drawn towards looking for a phrase that encompasses the whole domain of learning and change.

"I coach processes, I mentor people, I change perceptions" is what now sums it up for me.

The Low-grade Routine

There's a routine I use when coaching batting that involves a horizontal line of (about 6-8) static balls that the batsman steps to and drives then returns to a similar start position for the next one, then performs the same action on that one and each subsequent ball.

This, on the face of it, is an extremely low-grade routine. In fact I've used this from child beginners to adult players - and sometimes the non-verbal reaction from either player, or indeed parent, reveals a huge amount about their preconceptions of what and how to coach. Sometimes this spills over into the implied verbal: "I'm paying you to coach me (or my son or daughter) in how to bat better - not to hit a line of static balls into a net." **Then I have to explain what the exercise tells us.**

And this is why I like coaching children without parents close enough to verbally intervene, because the children just accept the instruction because they have no preconception of what the real purpose is. They learn by experience and not thinking - let alone pre-thinking!

So what does the exercise tell us?

* It tells us where the batsman's front foot steps to - past the ball, too much to the side, in the way of where the bat should be etc.
* It tells us the 'shape' of the shot, i.e. the 'flight-path' the bat traces before, during and after hitting the ball
* It tells us the balance of the batsman before, during and after hitting the ball
* It tells us what the batsman's head, shoulders, hips are doing in the course of the shot
* It tells us about their ability to replicate the starting position, and subsequent action of this closed-skill activity

There are other things it also tells us, but in the above-mentioned alone there is a huge amount of information - and all without even looking at where each ball has been hit to.

A very 'low grade' routine that reveals an abundance of very 'high grade' information. It's about what are we doing - what is the body doing - in the course of this simple activity, the focal point of which is that micro-moment in time when bat hits ball.

It is about PROCESS and not OUTCOME.

Now in coaching terms, understanding the balance between process and outcome - and then conveying that understanding to our clients and players - is about as simple or low-grade as the routine I've illustrated above. And yet it is the most crucial and pivotal factor in their ability to learn and change, and in learning HOW TO learn and change. And for most of us, learning is a process we are not taught how to do - it is built up in stages from our earliest steps and communications by experience and modelling.

Success

The success of each one of us is our own property because success is an outcome. Ability is the process we apply in order to achieve an outcome. A coach can be successful - but cannot coach success. Success belongs only to the clients, the players.

A player can have all the ability in the world, but if he chooses not to apply it, then he will not achieve his desired outcome in that context.

Plus - in the *Game of Life* we are ALL players.

So what was it I saw Andrew Strauss doing in the background of that televised footage?

Yes - you've guessed it - he was working with his batting coach on a very low-grade routine - hitting, one by one, a line of static balls into a net.

Remember to Breathe

Our cricket club's Under 15s side had a match one Sunday morning. It was warm, pleasant and sunny and our side had batted particularly well and there was little possibility of the opposition matching our score. This type of match situation gives our skipper the opportunity to involve the less regular bowlers in the game.

One of the lads at the end I was umpiring was struggling to relax and bowl with consistency. In amongst the good balls were "Wides" and his control was teetering on the very edge!

Earlier in the season he'd been in this situation before, but on that occasion I'd been watching from off the field of play so could only remark about it afterwards. I told him then about how much composure helps his accuracy when bowling and about how important breathing helps composure.

Back to this Sunday morning, and all I could hear from behind me as he came round to bowl the next ball was short and shallow breathing - almost panting - with an open mouth. After the next ball I caught his eye and said "Remember to Breathe!" He knew exactly what I meant and as he smiled his shoulders immediately relaxed. Everything went fine for him from then on and there was no more anxious panting.

Was this coaching while the game was in progress - something we frown upon as officials? Yes it was - though it wasn't coaching in terms of anything to do with the game. So my three little words said almost in passing had exactly the desired effect for him, and I had my excuse ready!

Breathing is so important in performance for relaxing the body and clearing the mind. When you are doing anything "under pressure" check your breathing first. Control it and it will then help control all that you are asking your body and mind to do.

The Silence of the Ticking Clock

"Between the lines of our thoughts are vast uncharted territories. Ask yourself this - can I free my Self enough to go there?"

I was doing a bit of one-to-one work with a young batsman which involved my feeding him tennis balls to hit – but with a fast repeat on the feed.
 I stood about ten metres away and fed six balls underarm in the time-space of between 6-8 seconds. For him, the exercise was to hit each ball as it arrived roughly back in my direction.

A fairly simple exercise, of course - and I've used it on many previous occasions to illustrate a number of things, viz:-

- The sharpness of his visual concentration
- How he re-sets into his stance after every shot
- What happens when he doesn't re-set to 'ground zero'
- What happens when he watches where he has hit the ball
- How light he is on his feet

- How integrated his stroke-play is with his body movements

These are what I would call the top 6 "outer" discoveries from such an exercise and there is much to notice and learn for both player and coach from them in technical terms.

- The depth of engagement, absorption and focus on the data of the moving ball
- His sense of balance when grounded in the stance
- His ability to hold the stance at 'ground zero' rather than inching forward after every shot
- His ability to disengage and progress to 'next task'
- His balance, agility and fluidity of motion relative to the ground
- His balance, agility and fluidity of motion relative to himself

With the last two, the stability of his head (and therefore eyes) is hugely significant - as is how his feet are making contact with the ground.

So that's all technical feedback which will help him advance and condition his technique, and move along the endless ladder towards Mastery.

Familiarity with the "Oh Dear" response

Of course everything and nothing does ever end there now does it? And we know - as with all things in life - that there is so much more that can get in the way when we are doing, when we are performing. Even in practice, like this simple exercise, we lay down our "pitch" using our beliefs about ourselves - beliefs based upon ???
Well, you decide!

We are not robots, even though we might consider that some of our abilities are robotic. We can make repetitive and robotic responses in countless processes, in the a la mode as illustrated by Tom Hanks in the scene where he plays Ping-Pong in the film *"Forrest Gump."*

Here's the thing though ...

Forrest Gump's outward abilities all extended from his inner ability, as some might call it, to disengage from his thinking.

The lad I was working with, in the simple fast repeat ball-hitting exercise, fell into the self-dialogue trap. Shots 1-3 all had good outcomes. Shot 4 had a poor outcome and his response (as I heard it) was "Ohhh" in a sinking and downward tonality. Shot 5 he missed the ball completely, Shot 6 he scrambled to play poorly (as it turned out) and more "Ohhh"s ensued.

Now we've all done this - and still do - on many occasions in the course of life's learning and conditioning. So what's going to help us most, at this moment in time, in terms of learning and moving on? Teachers, parents, coaches, friends, fellow life-players - all have a role to play here, as well as ourselves.

The trouble is that many of them, like many of us, fall into the self-same emotional and linguistic traps - traps characterised by "Ohhh" responses.

When babies are learning to walk, what happens when they fall over? For them there's no emotion in the act of falling - only a response to pain or discomfort after landing. They don't think "I can't do this, I'm useless, I'm rubbish, I'll never get the hang of this." For them, the thinking comes later. The irony is that they don't even use the "Ohhh" response either – their parents or elder siblings do!

And yet, although the baby's thinking comes later, the auditory familiarity with that ***conditioned response*** "Oh Dear!" starts at the same time as they become familiar with hearing their name. How we all code up such a phrase, in childhood, says everything about how we perceive it, re-code and then use it for ourselves.

Inner Learnings for Players

So we took a break and I talked to him about what is there for us to discover in the non-technical side of the ball-hitting exercise. I talked about humans and robots doing the same exercise, where robots are only as good as they are programmed and where humans are limited only by their propensity to distract themselves.

"Look how it started with the first 3 shots," I pointed out. "Focus was well directed, movement flowed, balls were hit, outcomes satisfactory, thinking nil!" He nodded in agreement.

"After Shot 4 there was judgement of outcome as being unsatisfactory - and then a response to that judgement with a behavioural response. We all heard you say 'Ohhh' and you also FELT something different on the inside compared to the first 3 shots. All of this - for you as a human - was destined to get in the way of the NEXT thing you were about to do, which was to play Shot 5. The robot wouldn't have had this problem for robot has no faculty of judgement or is able to remember. The next GoTo in his program would have executed as normal."

He smiled and, although I'd stated the obvious for him, he now had solutions placed in his in-tray instead of someone saying 'pull yourself together'.

Pull Yourself Together

Rather like the childhood coding of "Oh Dear!" or "Ohhh," we all have a coding of meaning in the phrase "Pull Yourself Together".

And yet, if we examine it robotically, what are the words saying here!?

There is a presupposition that "yourself", or your "self", is somewhat fragmented - is broken into a number of parts. The advice, in order to take the next step, is to bring these parts that were previously split asunder, back together again - to be re-integrated.

Now, telling someone to "Re-integrate Yourself!" would carry minimal emotion and a totally different perspective of advice - but there is an assumption in there that we (or the "I" we are advising) knows how to allow that re-integration to take place.

Self help begins when we know how to re-integrate; we can direct our own destiny beyond this fragmentation of self. And it is here where we particularly need to be on firm ground.

For my young player, it wasn't "Ohhh", but what went on just before that, that caused his distraction, that 'blew' his mind into enough pieces so that he couldn't apply his technical abilities to Shot 5.

So - what went on?

Shot 4 - the outcome was judged. He ran what he SAW as a result of his applied technique past his beliefs and in-built expectations, and gave himself a low mark - in the moment. Some thought-energy had been gathered to drive this process. The player's feelings and gasp of "Ohhh" came next, which were responses on the outside to what had happened 'on the inside'. And we can describe this as noticing our THINKING.

This exercise contained no instruction to judge the outcome - how or where the ball went to. It was merely to hit ball, return to 'base', hit ball, return to 'base' etc in a robotic style.

And he started out by doing just, and only, that! Then there was an error, a judgement, a breakdown, a blowing-apart. It is a very regular human response that is like the "Big Bang." If only we could learn to do the conditioning in a "baby-like" then we would learn much quicker!

We ran the exercise again several times, and he had great moments of absorbed thought-free engagement interspersed with occasional errors and one or two more "Ohhh" moments. It was good to hear him laugh after every "Ohhh" however, because in there he is abandoning the bonded belief that constantly judging his actions, like that, is always a permanent necessity.

Between the lines of our thoughts are vast uncharted territories

If you listen to the ticking of a clock, I'd invite you to notice the silences between the ticks. Focus on them and really get in touch with them. There's purposeful information in there.

And we can direct our attention using our R.A.S (our perceptive filter), to notice more about those silences - rather like we can use the R.A.S to direct our sensual attention to pretty much any where we might choose. Although it's not widely accepted, we can even direct our senses of smell and taste as well - and I speak from experience here in the process of "Like to Dislike" **

So - in terms of performing a program of sequenced actions - our thoughts, we know, get in the way of being able to best perform those actions. Between the lines of those thoughts are the profound stillnesses of the Flow State. They are, indeed, uncharted territories. We cannot describe them, we can only use metaphors to paint a verbal picture of what the territories are like - for us.

Yes, the clock is set to tick - but without the silences there is no tick. We only know the clock is ticking *because* of the silences!

And so, for each and every one of us going through all of life's performances there is really only one question we need ask:

"Can I free myself enough to go there?"

[** - Like to Dislike is the process of 'mapping' the sub-modalities of something we like onto the holographic location of something we dislike.
http://pjwhypno.blogspot.co.uk/2010/03/mapping-across-bye-bye-to-jaffa-cakes.html]

Where do you think you're going?

There is a famous quote by Henry Ford: "There are two kinds of people. Those who think they can and those who think they can't – and they're both right."
In sporting terms this certainly applies too, because there's thinking in there – and we always have a tendency to "act out" our thinking in the way we are being and playing!

If you've just been picked to play for your country, county, district, 1st team, club, school for the very first time – in amongst the pride, the sense of achievement, there probably comes that nagging reflection – am I good enough? Can I hack it at the next level?
And it goes right across the board -
Your club or team has won promotion. How will they fare in the higher league? Are they good enough? Do they need better players with more experience?

Even on life's stage I've encountered people who are up for recognition and awards and who are almost embarrassed and ask "Why Me? – They'll suss me out sooner or later!" I've also encountered people who have been head-hunted for highly rewarding jobs, and who are so concerned about their ability that they start getting stressed out because they feel they have to try *so much harder* to impress their new bosses that the right choice has been made, or that they are up to the job!

I know it sounds silly and illogical, but there is hardly a person anywhere on earth who hasn't plagued themselves with this thinking at some point in their lives.

This train of thought inevitably brings us back to Henry Ford's quote. If we think we can't do something, then we'll act out, direct our actions towards becoming the inadequate, the loser, the under-achiever. What fuels this action, what perpetuates this momentum?

Belief.

And what is a belief?
It is originally a thought that became > an idea, that became > a notion, that became > a concept, that became > a theory, that became > a belief. There's a kind of process of cell division that takes a thought to a belief, and for each step along that road we verify and prove – through referential experience – what we perceive as

'true' or 'real'. We know about what's real and true – or at least we **think** we do!

If we believe we *can* do something, then – along a similar highway – we'll prove it to ourselves. This will not only reaffirm our belief, but it will also bring us success!

So, to get back to the original scenario, where you've been picked to play at the next level up; There's a random thought – am I good enough? It's only a thought and you hasten, perhaps rush, that thought along the road towards the certainty of an **answer** at an accelerated rate.

Now if you think you CAN, and you have confidence in your abilities, your beliefs will filter your gathering of references in alignment with that confidence. Answer = Yes I am good enough. I *can* play at the higher level. Likewise, if you think you CAN'T then you'll draw out all the references that align with that belief also. Everything is clear, one way or another.

CAN - DOUBT - CAN'T

However, what about the vast grey area in between, when you are *not sure* – if there is *doubt*. You *want* to know – you *must* have the answer. "I *need* to know, which will give me confidence! Only *when* I have confidence, *will* I play in a way that gives me the answer and dispels the doubt! If I *don't* know, and *don't* have the answer, then I *won't* have the confidence to play in a way that *will* dispel the doubt."

Remember R D Laing's quote:
"If I don't know I don't know – I think I know. If I don't know I know I know – I think I don't know."
It's all a bit like that, and we carry those doubts and lack of surety into the playing arena! Then, any spare capacity left in our emotional bath, gets filled by "I *wonder* if I'll be OK," or "I *hope* it goes alright for me today," or "I must *try* my best," or other variations on a theme. We'll ponder when people wish us "Good Luck!" Maybe they're right – yes, I'll *need* luck too!"

There is nothing convincing about wonder, hope, try and need though, is there? Hope, try and need do a very good job of supporting our doubt – and if you think about it, that doubt, if unsupported, would collapse into can't.

And all we ever wanted anyway was to know – to be convinced, to be *sure*!

OK, let's break down this sample of rock and see what really lies inside!

Is confidence real, or just something we've made up – a construct?
Do I really need to know the answers to doubt before I play?
If our doubts are real, who is making them up?
Are beliefs real, or just thoughts, amplified and proven through experience.
Is experience real, or just our interpretation of events.
Are thoughts real anyway?

These are all questions about what is really real and, as we sift through them all, we'll eventually arrive at a point where we'll know the answers.
And, here's the thing – once we know our thoughts aren't real, then why would there ever be any need for us to pay so much attention to them and certainly to question our ability to play? Why would there ever be any need to take those thoughts onto the field of play? All we would ever need to do is to be enthused and excited by anticipating the play, and then to engage in

every moment of the play when eventually the time came.

It's a simple formula that requires you NOT to think about it, but merely to understand it.

The Book of Judgement

At the end of a coaching session last evening I was watching a lad bowling a tennis ball at his brother.
The first one went wide to the left - and the second one went wide to the right. There was plenty of huffing and puffing, shrugging of shoulders, and a chorus of "I can't bowl with tennis balls - they're so light."
It was an interesting array of excuses and beating himself up - all tilling and making fertile ground for seeds of self doubt to come along and germinate.
"So what," you might say - "we're human - we do that all the time."

The thing is, for us to have learnt how to beat ourselves up and make excuses, we must have had a teacher or teachers, from whom we have modelled our behaviours. At this point in our young lives we take our models as exemplars, and firmly believe this is the way the world is. We are not judges of their energies or wisdom, we just code up our experience with readings from their *Book of Judgement*; whether we are surrounded by those with a spirit of understanding, generosity and learning through experience, or whether we are surrounded by one-eyed perfectionists!

What happens next is that our own growing and expanding **Book of Judgement** - and its inherent hierarchy of values - is taking shape based upon our, understandably immature, comprehension of the nature of the data in our world.

We learn very young what happens when we cry out for attention, and also the kinds of expressions and responses we get from others when we are doing things and learning to do things. These are the building blocks of the way we are framing up our maps of the world. Consider the difference we might notice when someone says to us, "Do it again," compared to "Try again." The first is merely an overt instruction to repeat - whereas the second is a covert instruction to repeat plus a presupposition that a) we'd got it wrong, made a mistake and b) that we were trying poorly in the first place.

"Yes, but isn't this all common parlance?" you may ask. Well, yes and no - but whichever way you look at it there's quotes in there from someone else's **Book of Judgement**, not ours!

When the word "try" is employed and, with young ears,

we get to hear it a lot, we build an understanding as to what it means. We then take with us the idea that whenever we hear it, and whoever we hear it from - that it always means the same. So - what starts to happen when we hear it used in a phrase such as "try harder"? It's always said like that, too – not even "try some more", which is perhaps what the real intention is behind the instruction.

There's an interesting exercise you might do with a group of adults, which is to get them to demonstrate - in a physical way - what kind of pose and posture they might adopt in order to be seen to be **"trying harder"**. There's a tension in the bodies and limbs, a clenching of the fists and or jaw, and so on. Any relaxed or grounded state is probably the furthest away thing on view. And when we adopt this state and posture - what are the chances of us actually giving the task (mental or physical) our best shot?

So, for the young lad I was observing, his next effort after two "errors" was probably going to be framed in "try harder" mode. A good time for me to intervene!

"Joe, when you bowl, allow your front foot to land. That way you'll have stability. Sometimes when you bowl you release the ball JUST BEFORE the foot has landed - so you are only balanced on one leg. And when you are moving and on one leg your balance isn't as strong as when you are on two! Allow that front foot to land and ***notice what happens***."

Joe bowled, allowed the front foot to land and - Hey Presto - the ball went dead straight, exactly where he wanted.

"Cor," he said, "Pete, how do you know all the answers!"

"Ah," I said, "I don't know all the answers. I do know most of the questions, though - because I've seen lots of people bowl and there aren't that many questions!"

He laughed and carried on bowling, most of the time allowing his front foot to land - and knowing when he bowled wide that he probably hadn't allowed it to land. The other thing that may already have started to happen, is that some of the pages in his ***Book of Judgement*** have now been updated with a degree of objectivity that may begin to filter into other chapters, in a similar way as well.

In conclusion I would like to offer you two things to consider.

Have a good look at the words and quotations in your

own *Book of Judgement*. Are they useful for you in your life, or are there some that might need to be updated - especially if you've brought them with you from a very early age.

And, finally ... remind yourself that
Sport is fun – Sport is learning – Learning is fun -
Sport is life – Learning is life – Life is fun!

Confidence and the Leap of Faith

In another article I have written about the *"Magician's Mindset"*, and how taking this single-minded approach to what we do - especially in terms of a contest, a performance, or taking any action - is a choice that liberates us from the debilitating shackles of self-questioning and self-doubt.

In terms of an illustration for this I always use the scene from Indiana Jones, called the "Leap of Faith" – which can be found on You Tube as a short video. Indiana Jones is going along a secret passage and comes to a chasm which is seemingly un-crossable. It requires him to take a leap of faith onto the stone bridge that he cannot see until he sets foot upon it. Then he realises that it is hidden from view - camouflaged, by a certain visual perspective. In that moment all his self-questioning and self-doubt evaporates.

Blueprints

The thing about self-doubt is that it is like a stalactite or stalagmite, built up by drip-drip-feeding from failure, lack of success, non-success, shortcomings, the damning effects of "could do better", the fear of our inability to please others or ourselves. The other thing is that once it has grown in one particular place, then a pattern has been established (a blueprint if you like) that allows it to be replicated in other parts of our life.

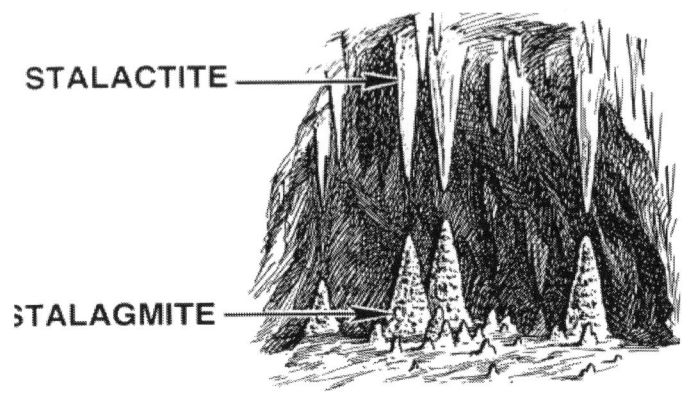

There is another blueprint - for self confidence, built in a similar way, and that pervades, by replication, other parts of our life.

And stepping back to take in the bigger picture, there are a whole range of blueprints, like a cave of stalactites and stalagmites. These are all forged and channelled by our various experiences and our RAS filtering, and we create and use them in all parts of our lives.

The Cache for speedy processing

These blueprints sit on the shelves in our chart-room along with all of our Maps of the World - waiting to be consulted for whatever we are doing, or are going to do. The thing is that the more we use certain blueprints and maps, the more we are likely to use them again and again. Rather like the 'cache' in our computer's memory, we keep these blueprints and maps close to hand for quicker processing. If we are 'good at confident' then we repeatedly continue to be good at it - likewise the pessimists, the moping types, the hypercritical ones, the judgemental ones reach for their same regular maps and blueprints because they're near to hand, and they continue to be good at being how they are too.

How do we talk about Confidence?

Look at these statements and decide which means more to you, which one reflects your beliefs more, and which is the most powerful for you:-
"I have confidence in myself"
"I am confident"
"I am self-confident"
"I have confidence"

Two statements relate to *having* - two relate to *being*; Two refer to just "I" - the other two refer to "I" and "self"; plus there's an implication that "confidence" is some kind of a tangible entity; and perhaps other linguistic nuances abound also.

The ebb and flow of Confidence

The thing about confidence, or being confident, is that for most of us it ebbs and flows through our lives and we tend to want more of it when we are approaching or anticipating a crucial or important event or action for us.

Most people ask me things like "I'd like more confidence when I do X" or "I want to feel more confident when Y happens". The requisition of more confident(ce) is needed in a certain context.

Then there's the people where the ebb and flow is less noticeable, where the tide is always low, and who just "want more confidence in my life" or who "want to be more confident in everything". Now these tend to be the folk who use **SELF** when describing what they want as well, and although this might be construed as being "just the way they say things", the fact is that they are also using SELF here - for a reason.

The late David Grove, the psychologist who developed Clean Language, also developed "Pronoun-scapes". There is something very interesting about how we break down the view of things relating to ourselves into the four categories of "I - Me - Self – You". This is so relevant, because there are ambiguities in the way we describe things about ourselves in this fourfold regard, that have a powerful hold over the way we draw and use our blueprints.

Take this conversational phraseology as an example:-

"You know, I find that one of the things that happens to me when I talk to myself is....."

How would YOU finish the sentence for this person? My reply is most likely to be:- "...that I don't really know who I'm talking to?"

Amusing as this may seem, once you start to listen out for how people use these pronouns when talking about themselves, it gives you some great clues as to what's going on inside their heads - and also clues as to how they can clear things up and move on.

So - back to Confidence!

It is a barometer - a readout in real-time – of how we feel about our ability to do something. Linguistically it describes, in an ideal sense, a way of being - on the inside. "I am confident!"
When we're confident, it's a way of doing actions when we don't have to worry or be concerned along the way about how things will turn out. It's a way of playing or performing when you know that through the processes the outcomes will be the best they can possibly be in each and every precise moment.

For all of us, getting to the state of having more Confidence is again about understanding the Leap of Faith - rather than relying on luck, superstition, drugs, alcohol, the quick 'external' fix, The Mask, The Tuxedo, the Invisibility Cloak, Sparky's Magic Piano etc.

In terms of Indiana Jones, Confidence is *faith* that the "stone bridge of processes" is what gets *You* from *Now* to the Outcome of the other side of the chasm. Yes you can be guided, but that step, that choice, the Leap, is something only you can do.

It starts by looking ourselves in the "I".

Impersonal

The Practice

I recently touched base with a young player (we'll call him Tom) whom I hadn't seen for about 8-9 weeks. In that time the season had begun and he'd been involved in quite a number of matches and practices at his own club and at school. Prior to that we'd worked together on a weekly basis through the winter, where – through his application and dedication – his skill levels, expertise and confidence had grown by considerable degrees.

His Mum had said to me, "Tom's not comfortable with his bowling. He's unhappy with what he's doing; the coaches at school have changed part of his technique," and so on, etc.

Now, his Mum's description of things was probably not his – but instead her interpretation of how he'd described it to her. Interpretations, such as these, are re-personalisations – and we all do this kind of thing perhaps many times a day in the course of our conversations and thinking. So, as we walked to the practice area, I checked out with Tom what HE felt like and what HIS thoughts were – and there was a marked difference between the two versions I'd heard!

Next, along with a number of other players, we just launched into a very informal practice session. Tom looked happy and comfortable enough, and as far as I could see the technique changes (ironing out a small, yet common enough, quirk) looked very well in place and established. And then he bowled a wide ball...and then he bowled a short ball...and out came all the negative body language!

"So what are you thinking right now?" I asked him.
"I'm thinking about getting it wrong," he replied.
"And what are you thinking about doing next?" I continued.
"To try and not do it, again."

Now this is a very regular and common conversational scenario for any coach. However, while these are very predictable answers, I'd invite you to consider what he might have said had I asked him, "So – HOW ARE you thinking right now?"
To be honest, as he's an 11/12 year old I'd probably still get the same answer from him – though, I might not.

There might be a pause, a gap in time, a space where he might go on an "inner search" for the words so his unconscious could assemble an answer to this somewhat different question.
I might casually put it another way, "So – WHAT IS your thinking right now?" The implication here is less specific – more along the lines of "tell me about your train of thought".

Curious, isn't it, how we might put (what is for us) a question to hopefully elicit a specific answer – and yet the person we're asking can interpret it in as many different ways as we can ask it.
Although I'm digressing slightly here, I'm inviting you to just consider the level of personalisation we are capable of bringing to any and all proceedings.

The practice continued, as did our conversation.

"Tom, can you change what's just happened, what's just gone?" I asked him, and he shook his head. "There's some useful information in those mistakes," I said, "but most of us are usually so niggled or upset with ourselves at having made them, that we never get to notice the useful information." He smiled, relaxing a little more. "The other thing is – as you have said – we

THEN start trying to correct what we are about to do next. How weird is that?" I asked. "Before we actually do the next thing we are going to do, we are already trying to correct it. Doesn't that mean we know what we are going to do – i.e make a mistake – and try not to do it?!" He was chuckling at this stage – a very nice unconscious response!

I explained to Tom what I could see from what he wasn't telling me verbally, and asked him to notice what starts to happen for him when he stops trying. "With the things your coaches have helped you change – the body, those muscles, they need time to adjust to doing things in a different way. And from what I can see, they've made all those adjustments very well already. All you need to do now is let them get on with what they do best – by not thinking about all of that. Just put your focus onto WHERE you want the body, those muscles, to put the ball when you bowl next. And the best way to do that is to put ALL your seeing power, your focus and inside attention onto THAT place. You can help that by switching off, or turning down other things to do with your senses - like, what you can hear and feel around you, AND that voice inside your head that is part of your thinking.

The linguistic level of impersonalising, especially his body, his muscles, was not done without purpose. So "your body, your muscles" becomes "the body, those muscles".

In my experience perfectionists are perfectionists, even in practice – and are very good at beating themselves up, and perpetuating that self-berating. By tinkering with the nature of THEIR own particular mind-body link, then changes of their self-perception can be brought about.

Yes I AM my body, but minds only think and bodies only act. The mind is where I see and think perfection, or imperfection. Bodies carry out actions initiated from the mind, and they need to "learn their lines", so to speak, when it comes to sequences of action.

Viewing the body as a separate partner helps "I" to realise that the errors, the imperfections, are perpetuated by the thinking in the mind and not the actions of the body. And that the responsibility for the actions lies with the thinking.

Good quality thinking = good quality actions; imperfect quality thinking = imperfect quality actions.

Calling practice – and their own particular practice – *work in progress,* can also open doors for players in this regard. Again it disengages the structure of "I's" thinking from their previously held propensity for making incessant self-judgements and demands of getting it right.

I'm pleased to report that Tom's body language and self-dialogue soon got into a much more grounded place, and he was then able to make a much better use of the conditioning nature of the practice session. The proof of the pudding is always when he is away from the 'comfort zone' of our session and in the different kitchens of practice elsewhere and – most of all – the cauldron of competition!

"The Zone"

This particular session was also useful for me on reflection – in regards to "The Zone", being in it, and how to get to it, and how to stay in it. For sports persons in particular it's a place where the level of detachment from thinking is total; where IMPERSONAL is at 100%.

It's always deemed to be the "Holy Grail" of performance, and as such there are many chronicles of *the search* for it! I'd invite you to consider this small linguistic artifice:-

I'M PERSONAL
IMPERSONAL

Now if we want to get to 100% Impersonal, where there are no breaks or joins in the word, then the level of thinking needs to be 0%. And we all know, because we've all been "in the zone" at some point in our life's performance, that our memory of such an event is that we were not thinking – just doing. Everything seemed to just flow with a thoughtlessly smooth quality. For some it was like watching ourselves from some detached place.

Getting back to :-

I'M PERSONAL
IMPERSONAL

The only visible difference is one apostrophe and one space; the pronunciation is different; but the letters are the same.

The moment we let "I" into our thinking there is a trade-off somewhere else. Percentage points start to drop off *Impersonal* until, if we are so inclined, we become completely bound up in our own "I" thinking and it becomes totally *Personal*. And we all know what happens when we take things personally, don't we! Do these sound familiar...?

What do I look like? What will they think of me? Don't they know who I am? She told me I was stupid! They said awful things about me! I want to make an impression! And that perennial classic, *I said to myself, you can't do this!*

So getting into The Zone is arguably a much more straightforward thing than the Holy Grail hunters would have us believe, and staying in it is not the feat of epic proportions we might have once thought it was. In essence - WE needs to get out of OUR thinking. It needs to become IMPERSONAL and then things start to flow. The moment we start to get in our own way by allowing "I" to get in there, the flow begins to get slower and stagnate.

To use another modality – stagnant water smells pretty rank. So if we want the sweet smell of success that comes from performing in The Zone, then we need to get the water flowing again by dredging out all the personal stuff.

Do 8 year olds think outside the box?

I was working at some cricket fielding exercises with a group of six Under 11 cricketers - and in particular I did a competition with them at throwing and hitting the target stumps from about 15 metres away.

After we finished this I asked them what is the most important thing to do when trying to hit the stumps, and they all echoed at once, "*We need to concentrate by looking at the target.*" - Pretty straightforward so far. Then I invited them to consider something a little 'outside the box'. "How good do you think you'll be at hitting the stumps when you throw with your eyes closed?" Some thought they stood no chance because they'd only managed one or two hits with their eyes open. Others (especially all the youngest ones) just took it in their stride, without even considering it was an 'outside the box' request.

We ran the same competition, this time throwing with eyes closed - with some hits and a lot of very near misses. Eventually after 2 rounds we had two contenders for a deciding throw-off. One was a young county player and the other was a beginner aged only 8

(though quite technically astute.)

The eventual winner was the beginner. I got them all in a huddle and then did something in the style of a post-competition "interview" with the winner.

"What was your secret to winning," I said. "What did you do specially so we can give your advice to everyone else here?"

Completely unfazed he said, "*I looked at the stumps as if I was taking aim, and then closed my eyes and threw the ball.*"

"Brilliant," I said. "And could you still see the stumps when you shut your eyes?"

He nodded.

The learning spin-offs from this little exercise are considerable.

All these youngsters will go away with:
* An uncomplicated belief that provided you take aim and trust your eyes then there's every chance of being successful.
* This spills over into what happens (a) when you try too hard and (b) when you just relax.

* When they encounter it properly, they'll understand that visualisation – which is precisely what this is - can be a very powerful tool!

For me it's a reminder that hitting targets is something we can do with our eyes closed! And, most of all, that at some point in our development we meet a 'box of conventionality' that rationalises our way of thinking about what is possible, what is the norm - and for some of us this conventionality is the carrier for limiting beliefs. There is definitely a glass ceiling here!

Clearly for this particular 8 year old there is no 'box' to think outside. He accepts everything as normal, there's a lack of anything called convention, and his ability to experiment, discover and learn continues unabated.

Long live Youth!

Decision Making

"Choices are the hinges of destiny" ~ Pythagoras

Within the structure of how we perform actions or tasks there needs to be a beginning.
I have a story about five seagulls on a pier and one decides to take off – How many seagulls are left on the pier? The usual answer I get is "four" – but I shake my head and say "five" The thing is, one may have decided to take off, but until he actually acts and takes off, then no action has yet happened.

"There is a distance between possibility and reality. Do you have the courage and the commitment to walk this distance?"
—Sadhguru

Here are some birds on a parapet. Some of them may have *decided* to take off – yet only one has *actually* taken off. This bird has flown beyond the mere decision making stage, into the next stage – the *action* stage.

However, it was after I was at a workshop once where the presenter asked us to consider how we might perform a task in terms of **four** stages, that I began to take a whole new and liberating perspective on the entire domain of decision making.

Here are the four stages:-

- **Making a decision to do the task**
- **Start the task**
- **Persevering with the task**
- **Completing or finishing the task**

The presenter next asked us to objectively mark ourselves out of 10 in terms of how we perform each of the four elements – and below I have illustrated the scores I gave myself.

• Making a decision to do the task	5-6/10
• Start the task	3-4/10
• Persevering with the task	9/10
• Completing or finishing the task	6-7/10

For me this assessment process threw up many learnings and understandings.

One of these was how and where procrastination makes an impact, as illustrated by only a 3-4 score. Another was that if we are in "doing mode" all the time, i.e. begin to do the task *before* completing the decision element, then our starting action is muddled with lack of total focus, accompanied by some score out of 10 of INDECISION or unclosed decision-making (in my case this was 4-5!).

So, with my score of 9 for perseverance, I am very diligent at sticking at the task once I've started. However, I haven't started with enough clarity of thought about all of the decision-making process – and this might be in the area of "how to do it".
Plus, would I start pushing up my finish/closure scores if I FINISHED the very first element (with a resulting higher score) BEFORE I actually started the task?

Consider this....

We've purchased a piece of self-assemble furniture.

Do we methodically lay out all the pieces and match everything up to the set of instructions? Do we read the instructions through and understand them BEFORE we start, or do we do this as we go along? Or do we jump right in and then have to make changes, backtracks as we go along – and then might be left with some screws, nuts, bolts etc at the end, wondering what we haven't done properly!

This is a very common pattern when the worlds of DIY and the male psyche collide!

Applying this entire Decision Making process to our batting.

I was coaching an adult cricketer who complained of having his *"head full"* and *"not having enough time"* to play shots at balls coming towards him. I began to work with him and observed that he was moving to play any shot he had decided upon far too early. Something was clearly muddying the waters!

I explained the four-part process to him and centred on what was happening for him around elements 1 and 2.

"Are you aware you are starting the whole action of hitting the ball (preparatory footwork and other physical movements) BEFORE you seem to have closed the element of making the decision as to what shot to play?" I asked.

He looked at me as if a light-bulb had suddenly come on inside his head.

"That's how I feel in a nutshell. That is exactly what's happening to me."

Next I got him to mark himself out of 10 for each of the four parts of the process, just as a bit of background and to also get him even more attentively engaged with the whole process of change I was building for him.

I then told him to face the next 10 throw-downs and not start the task of taking action **UNTIL** he had completely closed the decision-making process which is Part 1. I had an idea that he would probably find he had more time and a head much less full, though I kept this to myself at this stage! After this, he and I would then talk about what he felt was different for him.

He played the next 10 shots in a way he had not done previously, and before we even started to have a chat about it he started smiling with satisfaction. Clearly, he had noticed lots that felt different.

What he didn't realise previously was that the *"head full"* and *"not having enough time"* feelings were partly due to the attentive foreground of his concentration being filled with both deciding what to do, and initiating the action involved in that decision.

When we overwhelm our every present moment we get a sense of time being distorted in some way. Sometimes this shows up in the form of being so absorbed that we *"lose all sense of time."* At the other end of the scale this shows up in the form of *"I haven't got enough time, or I feel I'm running out of time."* This gives us the sense of time racing, leading us towards a form of panic.

Another part of the decision-making process involves our gathering information about the flight of the ball. The bulk of this information is gathered by visual means of course – as we watch the ball.
By delaying his starting to take action, he is actually watching the ball for longer, which results in the QUALITY of that gathered information being enhanced, thus making the decision being based upon better and more meaningful data.

In essence, this process improved his level of concentration and gave him a sense of still having plenty of time to play each shot.

Having polished up what was happening for him in Parts 1 and 2 of the process, he then noticed the sense that he was getting more out of each shot for less effort. This made the perseverance of Part 3 a far more effortless process. Finally – and for him the most significant part – the outcome of the shots was much improved. In other words, he now felt that he could score himself much higher for Part 4 of the process.

Working outside the Bubble of Expertise

Last weekend I coached 3 young district level cricketers for an hour each, and it was my first coaching at this level for the best part of two years. I have to say it was a real pleasure, both in terms of our interaction and their outcomes. Also I'm hoping that they'd gained enough ideas for change to stimulate and motivate them to taking their (batting) game onto the next level.

I approached them as clients, rather than "coachees" or (even worse) schoolboys, and looked to establish an atmosphere where they could express themselves. Although I knew all three, only one of them do I coach privately - and he is well versed in my 'atmosphere' of practice and experiment! The others (both aged 13) took a short while to become accustomed to the kind of freedom afforded to them, because essentially they are usually accustomed to being coached from a different perspective.

I spoke to one of them in particular about how learning something you like is not a chore but rather a pleasure - the very reason being *that you like doing it*. "Think of school," I said, "and the lessons in subjects you like. You look forward to them, you relax, pay more attention, and the whole learning thing has momentum before the lesson even starts."

The key action next is to capitalise upon this positive state and allow them to open up to all the possibilities afforded by what they are experiencing in practice. These possibilities exist outside the box (or bubble) of current expertise. Now, they could perhaps just want to 'groove' their current expertise - but that's not a learning experience, it is more of a conditioning exercise. And I wanted to engage them in learning (discovering) more about the breadth and limit of their capabilities by getting outside the bubble!

Interestingly, this bubble (or box) of current expertise is also the domain of the perfectionists and "finite-masters". These are the ones who are habitually prone to beating themselves up because they are trying to match what they're doing to their pre-conceived (and often perfect) model of their capabilities.
"I want to perfect what I'm good at, and **THEN** I can move on!"
Mmmm - so much for learning as you go; plus it makes for a stop-start-stop type of learning curve!

Sometimes I talk to players about the box or bubble and what happens when they're inside or outside it - and there's a great question I use for bursting the bubble of the finite-masters or perfectionists.

"Consider this - how did you get to be as good as you are already? There was some point - back in your past - when you weren't as good as you are now. So in order for you to have become as good as you are you must have allowed yourself to become better than you were!"

So, once outside the expertise bubble the chance for learning is down to experimenting, experiencing, finding out what works and what doesn't, noticing what's happening on a sensual level and on using outcomes only as a means for collating results of the experiments.

By the end of each of their sessions all these three lads had trodden some new ground. It was challenging going to these new places - but they were invigorated and enthused by realising that, through experience and experiment, when they came back to their 'bubble of expertise' it was now bigger!

Little wonder these guys are already much better than they were a year ago - and they are still capable of far, far more than they think they are. The difference is that now they have an inkling that for every new "Now" moment they experience they discover even more about their capabilities and, more especially, about themselves!

Suck it and See

There are many times in performance when our thinking gets in our way. The more we think - the worse it gets!

To stop people thinking so much (especially those within teams), particularly about the 'what ifs?' of techniques or outcomes, I get them to think tactically. It's a projecting and external process, taking them largely outside their internal dialogue and self-critical faculty.
A real help here also is deep and controlled breathing to get them grounded, calmer, and with more mental clarity.

I had a recent occasion to work with a young cricketer who, when batting, would move away from a ball that was coming straight at her. This is a natural protective or "flight" reaction carried over from a time when younger. As an embedded habit this is extremely common, and there are a number of ways of tackling it - the choice depending upon which is most effective for any particular individual.

In previous cases I have used anchoring, reframing, and inducing a 'sticky back foot' as a means of correcting the process of avoidance. For the young lady in question she described it as "finding myself thinking what to do when the ball was coming straight at me". Whilst this appears to be part of her shot selection process, she said she had no discernible "thinking" when the ball was not coming straight towards her.

I took a bit of a flyer here and saw the intervention of her over-cautious critical faculty as being the thing to distract or switch off. In terms of ecology, just watching the ball would be enough to tell her where any real danger lay, and she could rely upon this intuitive and autonomic process to protect her, to keep her safe.

As I said many times, especially in the book *"Don't Think of a Black Cat"*, to get her to **stop thinking** whether the ball is coming towards her or not is likely to fail at best! Instead I chose to give her something **ELSE** to think about - something in close proximity and kinaesthetic in sensual terms. (I chose kinaesthetic rather than visual because visual is critical to her shot selection.) I could have chosen auditory, but I wanted to keep that sensory channel free - for mainly technical reasons, both present and future.

First of all I got her to link a deep-breath sequence into various stages of the process of the ball being delivered to her. This is a very useful anchor for grounding and calmness and improves the shot selection process. Secondly I asked her to notice and consider what the tongue was doing within her mouth, through the period that the ball was in flight coming in her direction. This redirection of kinaesthetic information focus, and engaging thought processes to analyse what that tongue was doing, had an immediate effect.

I would like to add here that when getting her to direct and pinpoint her (kinaesthetic) focus I actually described it as "that tongue" rather than "your tongue". **"That"** tongue implies that the tongue is somehow separate from her and her control, and results in her noticing **even more** about what it is doing. This process takes only a few moments to talk through and set up, and involves the player in a degree of alteration of state - brought about by their 'going inside' (in this case mouth and mind). Sometimes I've called this process *"localised trance,"* sometimes I'm more comfortable describing it as *"moving perception around."*

It is a huge boost to a player's confidence to find that

(almost suddenly) they are not shying away from the ball, and instead they are staying more still and playing better shots as a result. This instant feel-good factor then adds into the loop and the process is enhanced every time they face a ball. The more they do it - the better it gets! In other words – **Conditioning**!

Using the tongue this way, or engaging parts of the mouth in other ways (such as gum-shield or chewing gum) is a good way of distracting over-active thought processes. By adding-in some subtle linguistic and mental artifices it all becomes much more powerful and effective.

Under the Radar

I was at one of the after school clubs I run yesterday, and before we started our cricketing activity I took the register – and then asked the group a couple of 'off the wall' questions.

I never pass up the opportunity to slip some kernels of ideas under the radar – because there's the world 'out there'; then there's the world we see, the world others see, the world we are all manipulated to see by society, institutions, advertisers, magicians etc. To be fair, there are an almost infinite number of worlds when we are dealing with the illusory worlds of our perceptions.

Reception and Perception

So you walk into a building and immediately you are confronted with that inner question, "where do I go?" Once you've got over the wide-eyed wonder of the all the variances of the place, then if you re not sure you'll be most likely to make for Reception. Of course, if you've been here before and you know where you are going, then you just make for the lift or the stairs. Once at reception you'll ask the Receptionist for help and directions and ... off you go!

When you enter the *building of life* – we'll call it the Worlds Building – then a rather similar process takes place. It starts with wide-eyed wonder, then you make for Perception and you talk to a Perceptionist.
When we are growing up, we meet our first Perceptionists at home and with our immediate family. After that we meet a whole variety of other Perceptionists as well. And this is how the whole conditioning process of understanding how the World works starts and evolves.

Are they proper Perceptionists though? We just don't know! Maybe they only know about one small part of the Worlds Building – maybe they have no idea what this is all about!

So, to get back to the original comparisons - if you are familiar with where you are going in the Worlds Building, then you'll enter and miss out Perception and make straight for the stairs or lift and head off to where you are going.

The thing is – the Worlds Building is an infinite and gigantic edifice, and you are just heading for one small part of it. What about the remainder?

Change

Perhaps you need to find another place because the one you know and have been going to for some time, is no longer doing anything for you; perhaps you want more out of life; there could be a whole variety of reasons for your desire for change.
Now if you don't have any idea that the Worlds Building is full of many different rooms, because your own thinking leads you believe that the rooms are all alike, then you'll feel stuck – and maybe you'll take life into your own hands, seek other – maybe drastic - solutions.
However, if you do have enough of an idea about the Worlds Building, then you can either wander around on a quest, a 'voyage of discovery' – or you can go and talk to a Perceptionist and get a clearer idea of where you might go next.

A Perceptionist can be like a travel agent, giving you a variety of destinations where you'll get a range of views of the world. The choice of destinations is yours – they have merely revealed the world of possibilities. Some travel agents might guide you (maybe manipulate you) towards holidays that they themselves like, or ones that pay them the highest commission. Some may only be able to show you a limited number of options. Here again, you won't necessarily know this. When you're going for change – the only thing you can really trust is yourself, your *intuition*. "I like the **look** of this one. That one **sounds** good. This **feels** like the right one for me."

Deciding which choice

The Perceptionist guides you towards the understanding that in the Worlds Building every room has a view; that most of the views are different; the windows are all of varying sizes. The travel agent will illustrate for you how your rooms are furnished and appointed; will tell you about meals, food and sustenance, and any particular local rules, requirements and protocols.

These are all things to help your decision ... and at the end of the day, it is **always your** decision. And remember even no decision is still a decision, and no choice is still a choice - as comedian Eddie Izzard illustrated with one of his mono-dialogues concerning the Spanish Inquisition. The choice was to be either ...

Cake or Death

Everyone was lined up and asked, "You – do you choose Cake or Death?" The answers were always **cake**, until the Inquisitor said they'd run out of cake. "So my choice is Or Death?" asked the next person. And at this point his narrative takes a huge sideways leap of comedic artifice. It's an amusing routine, filled with linguistic tricks, reframes and quantum perceptive leaps. Conversational comedians like Eddie Izzard are masters of "under the radar" perceptionism – and, for me, the Spanish Inquisition, Cake and Death will never again be quite the same way they were!

So, what of my group of receptive young cricketing minds –

Looking at the practicalities

As they were all sat down, I narrowed my eyes and looked up and down the line.
"What am I thinking at the moment?" I asked them. Many of them attributed their own personal

interpretation of my stare, and one in particular said I was "...thinking how naughty we all are, not being quiet or paying attention."

Very interesting, I considered. Clearly this answer was framed by classroom experiences of teachers with very much that thought in mind.

"That was the furthest thing from my mind," I said. "I could have bad eyesight and this is my best way of being able to see you all. I could have forgotten what I was going to say and was trying to concentrate and remember what it was. It could've been any number of things – but it certainly wasn't how naughty you all are. Judging," I said, "is a bit like deciding – you have to start with an open mind."

I then threw into the pond the well-known story of five seagulls sitting on a dock.

" I was on Ilfracombe Pier on Sunday and saw five seagulls stood on the edge. One of them decided to fly away. So – how many were left?"

There was a chorus of "four", which was predictable, and then one voice chirped, "Five." Everybody looked his way and so he elaborated, "one had only *decided* to fly away, you didn't say he had *actually* flown away."

I pointed out to them that deciding to do something is very different from actually doing that same thing. The England cricket team had, a couple of days before, been humbled by India in a World T20 match where, as I pointed out to the group, they'd decided to fly off the pier but when it came to the action they didn't fly – they just fell off the pier.

"In whatever games we play this afternoon," I said, "don't just decide to do something – actually do it! Do it with conviction, like you mean it. Then you'll find that you'll be more successful, AND the less thinking time you have between deciding and doing – the better you will be."

We then got on with the real business of just having some sporting fun; and the extra fun for me was seeing – on the radar of course - what extraordinary feats of performance emerged as the games unfolded.

Can you put it in a Wheelbarrow

I was working with a group of young cricketers and we were talking about hitting various types of shots and what to do with our hands and feet in order to best play these. Finally, I asked them the question that actually stands for ALL ball sports. "What is THE most important thing you need to do when batting?"

There was a thoughtful silence apart from the sounds of *brains in action* until finally a very bright 9 year old, probably the most talented young player I've yet encountered, blurted excitedly, "Concentrate!"
"Getting warm," I said, "So what is concentrate? I have a carton of fruit juice here with me. It says on it MADE FROM CONCENTRATE. Is it like that?" They all laughed.
"Better still," I said. **"Can you put it in a wheelbarrow?"**

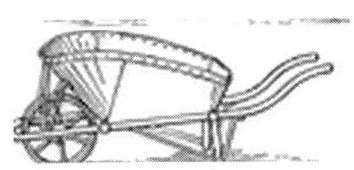

You know how kids tell you non-verbally when they don't understand and yet remain curious to know what it is you are talking about?
So I repeated, "**Can you put it in a wheelbarrow**? You can with concentrate for fruit juice - yes?
So what about YOUR type of concentrate?"

There was a bit of laughter and someone mentioned 'trick question' - and yes I suppose it is a trick question in a way. However this lad had already been tricked into thinking he knew about *concentrate* until some linguistic "NeLPer" like me started to redraw this particular 'Map of The World' for him! The fact he failed to come up with an alternative definitely meant he was echoing "coach speak" or "adult speak" without a full understanding of meaning.

Then one of the others said, "*Watch the ball.*"
"Exactly," I said. "Watch the ball. For us in cricket concentrate MEANS watching the ball, AND paying attention to other important things so we can best decide how to do what we want to do. If we don't watch and pay attention then we are guessing. Sometimes we'll guess OK, sometimes not."

As sports coaches (and in life in general) we often

nominalize a set of collective actions into one word - which we understand as "code" for that set of actions. However danger lurks in that nominalization because we can't "put it in a wheelbarrow", because (as it is) it is intangible. Think about words like concentrate - confidence - focussed - stressed out etc.

So how many nominalizations do you use, without REALLY fully understanding what they are code for? Have a ponder and notice what you notice - then ask yourself "Have I got the REAL and FULL EXTENT of what this is about?"

You may make some interesting discoveries! You'll certainly help broaden your perspectives and perceptions. And that's part of what NLP **DOES** - not what it IS!

What Happens when you do X?

A young cricketer I have been coaching for some considerable time has had issues with his batting - not so much technical, because I and other coaches have all coached the technical side of his game and he can play every shot in the book *when he chooses* to.
No, the problem is shot selection......*or so it would seem*.

How does the coach tutor shot-selection in any sport where the ball is moving towards the shot maker?
(A semi-closed skill - given that the ball is moving.)

Visible clues and cues, of as high a quality as possible and as early as possible, are the bulk of the incoming sensory information. The ability to filter out other external sensory data is hugely important.
Also hugely important to eradicate is random and distractive internal dialogue. However, given that most Internal Dialogue is a needless examination of our Thinking, doing eradication – like that – is an endless process. It is better to know and understand and IGNORE (filter out) irrelevant random and distractive Internal Dialogue. The only Internal Dialogue we should notice is the positive, instructive and focussed

comments, mostly geared to the **next set** of physical actions required (*keep watching the ball, move your feet etc*). But at that key moment of shot selection the critical faculty needs CLARITY – needs to be as clear of irrelevant data as possible in order to make the best choice. QED.

So here is the framework of his actions.....he seems to make 70-80% "good" choices but because of his associated footwork the "good" percentage goes down to below 20%. In matches he gets out easily, almost irresponsibly it seems, because although he knows what he should be doing he seems to be un-careful and uncaring of doing it.

No one who times the ball as well as he can, or can hit the ball as well as he can, deserves to be given up on - but coaches usually want players to at least help themselves somewhat! And thus it transpires that he developed into a coaches' *abandoned dilemma* because of involuntary and uncontrollable foot movements.

Having worked with Clean Language, in this instance I decided to go for an approach to the dilemma from the *CLEAN* angle.

We looked at his foot placements relative to a complete range of shots and relative to the level of committed power to those shots.

PW: "So what happens when you play this shot?"
Plyr: *"I play with power"*
PW: "And where is power?"
Plyr: *"In my hands and arms"*
PW: "And what kind of power is that power?"
Plyr: *"**Very** powerful"*
PW: "And is there anything else about *very* powerful?"
Plyr: *"I put everything into it"*
PW: "And what needs to happen for *very* powerful?"
Plyr: (Pause) *"I need room to play"*
PW: "And when **very powerful** and **room to play**, what happens to that foot?"
Plyr: *"It gets out of the way"*
PW: "And when less power, what happens to that foot?"
Plyr: *"It's not so out of the way"*
PW: "And is there a relationship between power and foot placement?"
Plyr: *"I suppose there is. Less power means foot is in a better place. More power means foot is in a different place"*
PW: "And for foot placement to always be in a better

place, what needs to happen for power?"
Plyr: *"Power needs to be less"*

And here I deviated from Clean questioning,
PW: "And can you control foot placement?"
Plyr: *"Probably only if I control power"*

We left it there as he was anxious to get back to playing against proper bowlers. Over the next and subsequent batting sessions we all noticed a marked change in his **power:foot placement ratio** and the improvement in outcomes. He was clearly integrating his control over the level of power and how it gave him control over foot placement.

NLP in coaching works extremely well especially in dealing with barriers that are difficult to break down. Using Clean Language as well, effectively opens up even more doors that are "locked" or just stuck.

Reframing the Critical Voice

A while ago I did a 2 hour session with a couple of young cricketers. These were guys I had coached many times before.
Technically I know their levels of expertise relative to their elite-aspirant status - and there is nothing technically to hold them back from achieving county selection prior to next summer. It is in the emotional and psychological areas where their issues lie, and so these were the areas of investigation I wanted to open up for them.

I laid out some basic issues surrounding reality and perception and challenged some of their currently held views. My gateway to this is usually the question "how many ways are there to get out of this sports hall?" Most people usually count the doors, windows and other sources of egress…and these lads were no exception!

Having established for them there were literally thousands of ways, we then looked at how reality is pared down by our senses and filters, through a process of deletion, distortion and generalisation, into what we then compare with our maps of knowledge and experience and then finally perceive as *"reality."*

Essentially I proceed to show them that whatever we may all think is "real", in actual fact each and every one of us is making that up!

Along the way, they each identified how their state of mind and how they *react* to events and (more especially) their own technical actions, all contribute to the next and subsequent actions in some way. *Ergo* a positively inclined reaction and frame of mind will lead to a better function of process and thus a better outcome.

They were both, primarily, victims of the effects of their own self-critic - which was manifested via a damning and earnest **inner voice**. Having discovered this helpful 'individual,' I showed them how they would be able to audibly reframe the voice to a degree where the earnestness became comical. This involved turning the *serious voice with gravitas* into the *helium voice with giggly laughter.*

We installed a number of other processes to help

maintain a grounded state, and they both discovered that mastery of themselves was now a significant step nearer. However, this was an unconscious discovery, since most of my delivered communicative intention was aimed at the unconscious.

Having seen one of the lads recently for another session I was able to observe some interesting feedback.

It turned out that after our original session he had gone to a county training session in such a positive and assertive frame of mind that he had almost surprised everyone but himself in the way he was now performing.

In addition to this, his other sporting activities also had taken on a new positive mental framework. His father was amazed and delighted at his new approach, whereas the player himself was quite matter of fact about it all.

What I know, though I didn't reveal to father or son, was this:- Having liberated him from the constant self-appraisal and the vocal effects of damning and earnest self-criticism, he is now able to fully express himself with total confidence – and also take self-possession of the changes that have happened in his behaviour and responses!

And this IS liberation for him, because he can now move on to the next part of his road to mastery, his games have gone up a level, and now the work on a new set of technical and psychological issues starts in earnest – along with a whole new understanding of what earnestness REALLY is!.

Keep Your Conscious Clear

I was working recently with a 15 year old cricketer, and we were coming to the end of the session so I spent quarter of an hour with him on throwing at targets.

First we just explored *dead aim*** from about fifteen metres and he got the usual hit ratio as a start.
** [Dead Aim is a technique for laser-focussing on a point on a target. In sport it came from Golf, and in the history of Man it came from the best of the hunter-gatherers!]

After a little advice on improving various technical points he and I then had a competition (hits out of 10 throws). The most he got was 2 but with a much improved accuracy level. On one set I got 5 - but I explained that I'd been a *dead aim* devotee for about 4 years, and I also had practiced the facility to shut out distractive elements from the foreground of my conscious mind – which is, of course, my **Attention**.

To conclude the session I asked him what success level he thought he might have with **eyes shut**. Now, from past experiments and experience* I know that some players with good visualization can actually hit targets as well with eyes-shut as they can with eyes-open.

He was confident he would hit 3 out of 10 - which was more than his eyes-open score. So, he proceeded to visualize, open eyes, visualize and test for strength and clarity; and then when he was ready I asked him to throw with eyes closed.

He hit the target twice in the first three throws!

He continued, but had no more success - and so I asked him if he noticed what was going on inside his mind *after* the first three throws.

It turned out he had been thinking (a) how amazing this was for starters and (b) could he keep it up and then (c) he started thinking about why he was missing until (d) he was quite disappointed he had scored no more hits.

I explained to him that for the first three throws he had not done any thinking, but had only visualized the target and thrown without attachment or distraction. Thereafter when he returned to use the visualization this had begun to de-focus due to internal dialogue. The chance of his making any more hits thereafter was almost nil whilst the original process was being degraded this way.

Had he reset the visualization from the beginning, and been able to switch off that internal dialogue - or even dampen it down - then he would have probably had even more success.

* - [refers to a past experiment with group of players doing eyes-open and eyes-shut target throwing.

You can read about this experiment online at http://prodigycoachcoachesforum.myfastforum.org/Visualization_in_action__about19.html

The Clasped Fingers Trick

I was coaching cricket in a Year 4 class the other day and encountered a lad who was unable to hold the bat correctly. Well I say 'correctly' - in actual fact he'd got his hands 'crossed'! His dominant (writing) hand was at the top of the handle and 'weaker' hand was below, forming an 'X' as they crossed just above the wrist. When I asked him to change his hands over, he did so - and at the same time he moved his body and changed his feet around so he was now shaping to bat left handed - plus his hands had now reverted to being 'incorrect' in terms of being crossed.

The thing is, batting is a two-handed function, and there are very few shots he could play with his hands configured the way he was using them. However, after I ascertained he wrote right handed, I got him to stand the 'right handed' way and also configure his hands the 'correct' right handed way. So far so good - until he said *"I can't do it this way - it feels all wrong."* He was, it seemed, quite stubborn and adamant about how wrong it felt!

Whilst I knew he would eventually (with persuasion)

get it to feel more comfortable and 'right', the thing is this would need time as there was resistance to him trying to get it through experience and feedback alone - and I had around 29 other children to coach and limited class time in which to do it. I had to use some kind of persuasive trickery to break down his kinaesthetic feedback when he was using his hands my 'correct' way.

Hypnotic artifice

I asked him to put the bat down and clasp his hands with each finger alternately intertwined and with one thumb over the other. I showed him how I did it and asked him to copy me. He did it quite conventionally for a right handed person (right thumb over left). I then asked him to do it "the other way" - ie finger by finger and left thumb over right.

"How does that feel?" I asked him
"Different," he replied.
"Is it uncomfortable?"
"No - just different."

"Now I want you to tell me when your hands start to feel uncomfortable again. Any time you feel like you did

before just tell me. OK?
Now just keep those hands clasped like that (left thumb over right). Now turn those clasped hands so the back of that left hand is on top. Now just pull those hands apart sideways and hold them apart by about one hand's width."

He did just as I said - and then I handed him the bat handle to hold without changing how his hands were configured. I continued to talk to him while doing this - checking whether he was feeling any of that 'uncomfortable' feedback he was getting before, which he wasn't.

"Now you're ready to bat - OK? All you need to remember is that clasping your hands is really easy to do - and holding the bat is just as easy to do. And the more you clasp and the more you hold, the more comfortable it all becomes."

Within a few minutes and in the midst of a high-activity game situation, he hit the ball very hard and sweetly past me, with total ease and perfectly correct hands on the bat handle. I was very enthused!

Conclusion

There are a lot of tricks with the hands that can be really useful when confronted with seemingly "no-go" situations like this, and I've used a number of these from time to time. I would describe these as hypnotic artifices, because a) the subjects are watching what they're doing, often quite intently and certainly with a level of engaged conscious absorption or focus in what they are doing; b) there's kinaesthetic feedback which is telling them to also keep checking for another feeling that they, until recently, felt quite strongly. In my experience, this is the part of the action that releases them from the internal dialogue of "can't do it" - because they are comparing and judging against their own calibrated level of previous discomfort and awkwardness, by waiting for a feeling to come that never does!

Transformative - definitely! Cunning? - not really. (Well maybe just a little!)

The Power of Now

Quite often I find myself pondering on how we perceive time in its various forms, and how we understand the 'currency of time'. Rather as with money, this fuller understanding of time as a 'currency' helps us spend it with more wisdom.
When writing about "The Iceberg of Language" in the book ***Navigating the Ship of You*** I even describe Time as being one of the inner languages of our senses.

Time is a very spacey concept and I believe that the more ways of looking at time we give ourselves when we are young, the greater the understanding we have of how (a) we fit into time outside of ourselves, (b) we can manipulate our perception of time within ourselves and (c) how time intervals have a bearing upon our sequenced thoughts and actions.

Like most things, we first come to getting an understanding about time from our parents and older siblings. Through this understanding and multi-modelling process, we form our own perceptions of time and how we run our lives relative to the past-present-future continuum, time intervals and sequenced thoughts and actions.

The Importance of Now

Recently I was coaching a group of young players all aged 10 and under - and at the end of the session, after a very exciting game, they all sat down and I just recapped what we'd been doing, and how they'd all fared etc. Finally we went into a short 'Q & A' to finish the session.
This is usually where the children ask questions ranging from something we've just been doing to just about anything else. It's all conducted on a very quick and snappy basis by them and me, and it's a good way to spend 60 seconds or so of final interaction. Often interesting remarks bubble up to the surface, and this time was no exception.

"What Time is it?" asked someone, and as I glanced at my watch I couldn't resist responding with the famous quote from Yogi Berra, *"You mean NOW?"*

Curiously, a level of quiet fell over the group, and it was one of those occasions when you always wished that the 'cameras are rolling'. I grasped the opportunity and continued:

*"The Time is **Now**,"* I said. *"On my watch it's always **Now**. Yesterday, or earlier, has gone. You don't ask someone 'what time is it ten minutes ago' do you? No you ask about **Now**. Tomorrow, or later, has yet to arrive. When it does get here it will be **Now**. Only **Now** is right **Now**, here and now. And Now,"* I said very slowly, *"is the only place to **Be**."*

It was literally one of those timeless moments, as I could almost hear the words landing in their collective unconscious.

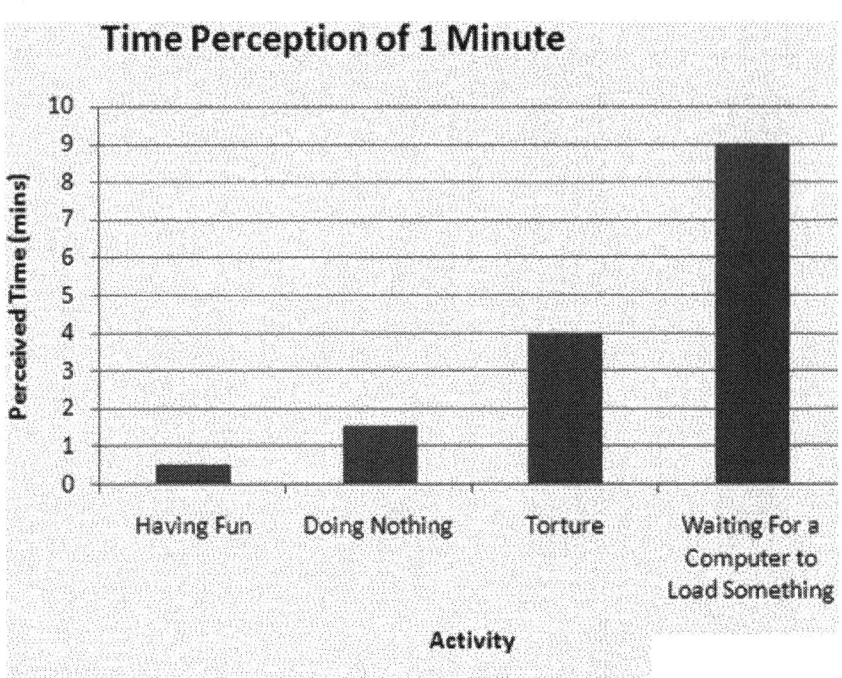

For most people, time is a real and almost tangible thing. Amusing as this graph is intended to be, it illustrates very well how we unconsciously 'bend' time, how the currency of time has a different value depending on whichever "land of the Now" we are residing in.

Controlling Our 'Tide of Time'

Of course most of us have heard of the saying *"Time and Tide wait for no Man."* It is one of those phrases handed down that relates to the very real and tangible nature the sea and the tides. We cannot avoid the REALITY of the tides.

A lot of the time though we just get carried along by our mental perception of the unfolding of time - "the tide" - without realising that "the tide" is something WE CONTROL, not something we are CONTROLLED BY. And that is the subtle point I wanted to make for the children.

When we are not ***In The Now*** we are either 'living in the past', or putting off our preset lives for something in the future. These are the "I'll be happy when..." people.

Some years later I was coaching an older group that contained one of the lads from that Under 10s group; and he clearly remembered the "NOW" episode.

As one of his team mates called out "What time is it?" he answered "Now," before I did.

We need to watch out for the language we use in the company of children – for we never know, now in the moment, how and when this is going to be modelled back to us in the future!

Weaving Spells with Localised Trance

Weaving spells: hands and arms, legs and feet

For some time now I have been using *'localised trance'* to coach the technical side of batting in cricket. Now this isn't trance in the sense that those that I'm coaching are *hypnotised* or, to use a phrase most people are familiar with, *"put under"* – perish the thought!
Clearly this wouldn't work – no, this is using what is linguistically labelled as *trance* from the following premise:-
For every conscious experience, we are in a particular state (frame of mind, balance of consciousness), and as that state shifts throughout our waking experience then each **change** of state involves our moving into a **'state of alteration'** or – put another way - an **'altered state'**.

Previously I have used this methodology in the course of coaching a number of sports, and it was only once I became a practitioner of hypnosis, did I fully understand the nature of states and the opportunities available when those states are in a process of flux or change. Once I began to follow the work of James Tripp and his exploration with what he has called 'Hypnosis without Trance', I found that it opened doors to endless opportunities.

As I see it, coaches now have a 'label' for what is taking place in terms of both micro-techniques and macro-techniques, and that further exploration can only take this process forward and start to gather pace. Part of my curiosity with 'Hypnosis without Trance' therefore is to pursue this exploration

Educating the body

The 'mechanics of batting' in cricket is all about educating the body in understanding and executing both major and minor motor movements with the head, arms, hands, shoulders and feet. These mechanics are then used, in conjunction with critical judgement of the characteristics of the ball in flight, to bring about the execution of any particular shot.

This is actually the structure used in any sport involving striking and catching a ball (or any object for that matter). In football for instance, these mechanics are executed by kicking, chesting or heading the ball; in bat or racket sports the 'striking implement' becomes an extension of the hand or hands, and the education here involves the hands, duly freed up by unlocked elbows, manipulating the implement to best effect.

A particular session

I had a session with a 10 year old player primarily in order to help loosen her wrists, elbows and shoulders thereby freeing-up her ability to strike the ball with better control.

I started by asking her to swing the bat and play some imaginary shots. Her 'top' hand (the hand at the top of the handle) started off in a good position but at the moment of striking and the follow through afterwards this hand in particular looked extremely out of position and uncomfortable. I got her to play the imaginary shots one handed with a lightweight plastic stump.

I asked her to *"notice in your starting position you can see the back of your hand. Watch the back of that hand as you are playing in slow motion, and as you do, pay attention to what is happening to the back of that hand at every point along the way."* I then got her to watch me doing the same thing in slow motion. *"Pay attention to what you are doing compared to what I am doing. Now gradually speed up what you are doing, still noticing the back of that hand and just allow your other hand to gently hold the stump and start to work in partnership with the other hand. Notice how different this now begins to feel compared to before."*

Very soon she was swinging smoothly and freely from the hands and wrists, and the elbows and shoulders just appeared to have opened up automatically and now also had much more freedom of movement. I exchanged the lightweight stump for her bat and the action continued to work well.

I then laid a row of static balls on the ground and asked her to step forward and hit each one in turn. Her foot movement was bizarre, as she lifted it in the style of a prancing horse!

So I asked her to show me how she walked down the street – noticing as she did how high her feet came off the ground. *"Now, when you step towards each ball I want you to step only as smoothly and comfortably as you do when you are walking down the street."*

This nailed it – and the end of the exercise was to go about 15m away and throw some balls down for her to hit and see now how she was doing it both in the step of the foot and on the movement of the hands.

Setting up and using a chain of small state-changes

This is a fairly standard approach I make for players who have issues with either their hands or feet. The thing is that this method sets up a chain of changing states, very localised, in the hands and feet. Added to this is the instruction to "notice" and "pay attention" to what parts of particular limbs are doing in the course of some slow motion action.

Part of the noticing instruction involves the **visual**, part involves **kinaesthetic**, and the RAS ** is focussed to gather this sensual information. The player is now building an experience of competence at an unconscious level by my guiding them to utilise these altered states by getting them to focus on what is happening on both the inside (kinaesthetic) as well as the outside (visual).

[** - RAS – is the Reticular Activating System, which is situated in the Brain Stem. Amongst brain functions such as moderating consciousness, it is recognised as the perceptive filter.]

Using the 'walking down the street' analogy as a means of correcting this player's 'pranced step' is again far more effective than most other methods. Firstly it gets away from any "don't do that – do this" instruction, which I always avoid because of the "DONT"; secondly I'm getting her to engage with a relaxed and natural process – just walking down the street.

In order to show me how she does it, she has to go on an inner search for a long-embedded and now autonomic process, and then 'get into a state' of walking down the street. So immediately she experiences an alteration in state.

While she is passing into this altered state, she is noticing, by focussed attention, how her feet are moving relative to the ground and the rest of the body. Here too there is visual and kinaesthetic sensory input. It is literally one small step from this experience, to replicating it when stepping towards and striking the ball. I have found that in most instances this method of correcting the biomechanics of stepping towards the ball works once and forever. Why? I think it is because, once again, the correct action has been installed unconsciously while the player was in (or entering into) an altered state.

Farewell to conventionality

I could of course coach this conventionally by getting the player to perform endless repetitions of the motor actions. And in doing so, yes the actions would pass into muscle memory and eventual unconscious competence. However, using localised trance and the nature of altered states, means that players can advance quickly through laborious processes and start to get down to the REALLY important part of striking the ball – timing; through the development and improvement of judgement using hand-eye co-ordination.

I have even used this methodology on players with dyspraxia and achieved excellent results. It seems that because the programming that runs the motor movements has been installed unconsciously, the brain is able to run the programme in a much better way.

Another benefit I have experienced by using this way of installing technique into the unconscious mind, is that part of this seems to become 'hot-wired' into autonomic functionality. I have seen dramatic changes in players from one week to the next, knowing that they haven't spent time practising the technique in the intervening days. Their unconscious mind seems to have done all the background processing necessary to raise the level of competence quite dramatically. This is what might be deemed to be *"**unconscious learning without having to practice.**"*

There is clearly more to 'unconscious learning' than meets the eye – (and hands and feet!).

Piling Everything onto The Learning Curve

Everyone talks about the learning curve ...
"So where are you at on the learning curve with this subject matter?"
"This is going to be a steep learning curve for me!"
"I'm not making any more progress with this – my learning curve has flattened out."
And so on.

Now I've written many times regarding the learning cycle – which I would illustrate thus:

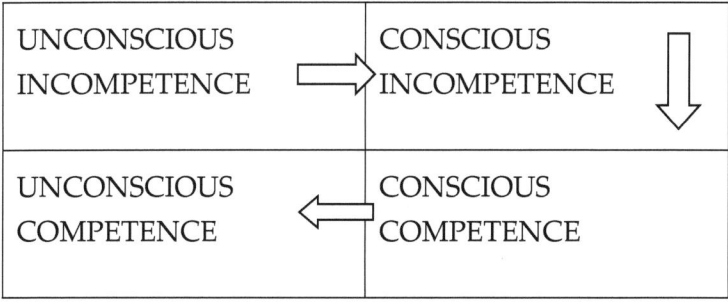

This is a cycle, however, and there is no plotting of our progress from Unconscious Incompetence to Unconscious Competence, against either Time or Numbers of Attempts at mastering any particular thing.

Then someone, at some point, plotted a graph of

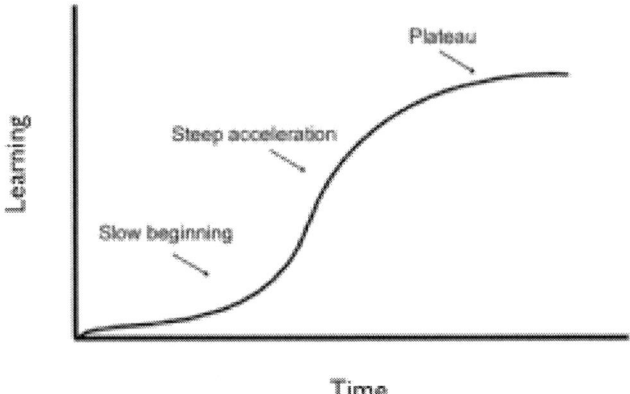

proficiency against time and called it a **Learning Curve.**

They perceived that graphically it was not a straight line, but rather more a line with a shallow gradient at the beginning, a steeper middle section and a final levelling off into a plateau.

Then, like all constructs, a number of things began to happen.
Derivative graphs emerged, plotting points against different axes. However, for me, the most important emergence was the idea that this entire graphic representation of the progression of human expertise became an accepted **NORM**. It took on a life of its own and became the benchmark of TRUTH for everyone.

Practice

As we know, there are many ways we might get better at something – and for some of us, the number of attempts, or the length of time we have been doing something has nothing **whatsoever** to do with our progress. Once again, part of that accepted **NORM** that society, educators and other people judge us by, is underpinned by the spoken myth of
Practice Makes Perfect.
Here's the thing about **Practice Makes Perfect** however– **NO it doesn't!**
Some of us attempt to do things for many years and still seem to portray the same level of incompetence we started out with. **WHY?**

The judges would have us believe that we just aren't cut out for this; or that we are poor learners; or that we are inadequate in some way; right down to the vernacular of the most "street-wise" of all judgements –
We're just plain thick. The "World" writes us off.

Yet, what if we <u>knew</u> that ONLY **"Perfect Practice Makes Perfect?"**
That's a bit of a gamechanger isn't it?
Here, now, is knowledge that doesn't write us off – this falls in line with the idea that **we are all capable of everything** doesn't it. All we now need to do is to find ways of bringing **Perfection** to our approaches to **Practising**. With this approach to practice we can now bring a higher level of Quality to our gaining of proficiency.

Yet – when all is said and done – we still find ourselves just tinkering with the **Learning Curve**; perhaps changing some of the gradients; perhaps arriving at **Unconscious Competence** sooner than we might have previously done. We are still piling everything about this gaining of proficiency onto just the ONE curve.

However, the whole idea of bundling all our perceptions of **getting better** at something takes on a new lease of life when we adjust our perspectives, our ideas, around the gaining of experience, of learning, of practice and of Performance.

I've found, in the ways I work with clients of all ages, that we'll only ever be working at any time on **ONE** of three areas –

Learning, Conditioning and Performance.

Now here's the thing - when we deal with *just one* of these in isolation it is a whole lot different from dealing with them even in tandem – let alone ALL THREE AT ONCE. I have found that this is a far better way of coaching – principally because of how we ATTEND; how we manage our ATTENTION.

It is probably down to the whole **Multi-Attentional** thing which we, as humans, seem to believe we can do and yet we fail at dismally.
"Oh, but I CAN multi-task, Pete. Watch me!"
And I watch, and yes, he can multi-task!
However, he – like the rest of us - CANNOT do multi-attention.

Multi-Tasking and Multi-Attention

Grandma, knitting whilst listening to music on the radio and talking to her grandchildren is a very competent multi-tasker. Her hands, while knitting, are on auto-pilot; she is looking at the children whilst her ears are listening to the music. She is visually attending to the children and the rest of her focus is diffuse.
When she comes to a bit of complex knitting technique she attends more to that **in the moment** and much less so to the children. Perhaps she listens more to the children **in that moment** than she does to the music, as a trade-off. Whichever way she does this, in reality, she is MANAGING her multi-tasking.

In any ONE moment in time, we can only attend to ONE thing. If our attention is elsewhere, then we are dividing our attention.

Perhaps the worst example of dividing our attention is when we are on our mobile phones when driving. And if you believe anything to the contrary, then I would suggest that when you ARE dividing your attention between the road and reading or sending a text message, your Unconscious Competence as a GOOD driver is now delusional and, in all truth, you have reverted to being Unconsciously Incompetent! Or, in other words, you have no idea how bad you are driving!

The Conditioning Curve

One of the things about any **Learning Curve** is that it should ONLY be about our learning. However - we have this propensity to map onto our **Learning Curves** the co-ordinates of another entirely separate curve - The "**Conditioning Curve**".

In the "doing" sense, our learning is merely about discovering and doing something we have never done. Conditioning, on the other hand, is about getting BETTER at it through repetition.
Think about going to the gym and/or getting fit. We engage with a set of routine exercises that we work at to condition our bodies to becoming more able to deliver a level of consistent athleticism. We aren't really learning anything, though, are we?
We may occasionally start a new routine – and we will become familiar with it. This isn't learning though, it is merely altering the parameters of our Conditioning. In terms of our fitness, we will also be able to plot our

proficiency against time or number of attempts (visits to the gym.) This is our *Conditioning Curve.*

When we judge our progress along our Conditioning Curve, we have an entirely different perspective as to what is happening in terms of our **competence**. Shortcomings are down to fluctuations and changes in our health, our lifestyle, our ability to regularly attend – in fact a whole range of reasons that have no bearing upon our skills, competences and abilities to LEARN. Does this make sense?

The Conditioning Curve is much more about **Practice Making Perfect** than the Learning Curve – yet here, too, Perfect Practice is also a very key element. The other things about the conditioning curve is the dependence upon our attendance to the action. The Conditioning Curve falls away when we don't attend to the action over time. If we stop going to the gym or exercise less – for whatever reasons - then our fitness falls away.

Conditioning is the repeated action of usage. Fitness is NOT competence. Stop putting fitness on the Learning Curve and let's free ourselves from the lack of clarity we get from muddying the waters of judging our data!

The Performance Curve

Oh, yes, and in case you wondered – there IS also a Performance Curve.

We can learn how to do something; we can condition ourselves to be able to consistently and repeatedly do something; and when we are then asked to go out and perform that something, we are then subjecting our ability and consistency to that thing called …
Performance.
We may have reached Unconscious Competence on the Learning Curve, we may have reached a good level of fitness or consistency on the Conditioning Curve – and now we are on a Curve of a very different kind!

When I work with clients on their **Performance**, in an ideal world we would pay no attention to Learning or Conditioning. We look, instead, at the Relationship with our Thinking, and how that affects our Equilibrium and our Temperament. This in turn affects our ability to manage our Concentration (our Attention and Focus), and our Decision Making. All these, conclusively, become synthesized into something we might label as **Experience.**

Experience is a construct that becomes more **tangible** the better we use it. In that regard, it is very much like **Confidence** – which also becomes more tangible the better we use it. Neither of these two constructs can be bought over the counter, or put in a wheelbarrow.

When looking at our **Performance Curve** for anything in particular we notice that it fluctuates.

Performances fluctuate.

The curve does have a bottom line – and the over-riding factor that plays into that base or ground-level of performance is our level of applied **Experience**. This is the tangibility I talked about just now, when we use our Experience well. Some people might even describe this by saying – **"We are Learning from Experience."**
We know, equally well, that if we do not learn from our Experiences, then our Performances will never get better – or we will never raise our level of consistency in performance.

How do we Learn from Experience?

Good question!
However, we need to be aware that in addressing this

question we have now left the Performance Curve behind, and are back on a Learning Curve!

We know that Experience is a construct made from a synthesis of our **Thought Relationship, Equilibrium, Temperament, Concentration and Decision Making**. And we will have a **Curve** that depicts how we are **Learning from Experience.**

We will LEARN from our every Experience from every Performance, by examining just and only those aforementioned 5 things! Our **Thought Relationship, Equilibrium, Temperament, Concentration and Decision Making**.

In fact, the more Grounded and Objective we are, the more we understand that the primary element (our Relationship with our Thinking) will provide all the answers for increasing our **Learning From Experience**.

So how does the baby learning to walk learn from experience – for he or she learns very well – AND – very fast!
Well, in terms of synthesizing **Experience**, baby is not weighed down with a relationship with his or her thinking, and temperament also plays little part in

proceedings. Baby is in a state of Equilibrium of Performance, is concentrating and is acting intuitively; baby is awakening to something it intuitively knows how to do though has not yet got an awareness of. Baby is gaining that awareness through Experience – which is PURE Learning.

We learn from experience by gaining an awareness that leads us to understanding.

Conclusion

So, the next time you hear yourself – or someone else – use **The Learning Curve** as a label, check WHICH curve is actually being talked about!

For in my coaching experience, once we differentiate between Learning, Conditioning and Performance, then we can really start to get very much better at ALL THREE – by making sure that we are not trying to Multi-Attend to those elements.

Watch Your Own Performance

It's a noticeable thing that generally, and in sport especially, watching a video of ourselves in action will often have a considerable effect on how we can best start to perform that action in a different way. Uncomfortable as it might seem at first, we often take the opportunity, when it's thus presented, to become more objective and analytical about the "us" we are watching. It's a very good way of honing skills, because within the video facility is the means of slowing down the film, in order to break down the various elements of a complex action into each link in the chain.

As a coaching aid within sport, video is a massively useful tool, both for players and coaches – and an astute and watchful observer can pick up an enormous amount of useful information about skills performance and also competition strategies. However, powerful as video might be, it is still just an audio-visual experience. In sensual terms it is 2 dimensional. Its abiding effectiveness lies in the fact that most of us within sport are visually oriented – i.e. we primarily work best at coding up visual experience and re-presenting it to ourselves in a similar fashion.

Realities

However, we are not robots – each and every one of us is unique. Not everyone is primarily visually oriented. In sensual terms we each make meaning of our experience in different ways, and across the sensual spectrum we each code up our experience in different ways as well. We are very good at recognising patterns, and this makes generalising a straightforward and common human propensity. We'll regularly say that Fred is LIKE John, Ellie SOUNDS like Pam, and William BEHAVES similarly to Pete. In the detail though, there is no generalisation because Fred may look like John but he sounds and behaves in a completely different way – as do we all.

So, given the uniqueness of our various realities, is there a facility where we can add more sensual dimensions into observing our performance?

On the outside, the use of virtual reality has been a real advance. Starting with flight simulators right up to now, with adaptive motion software devices such as the *Wii*, we are able to replicate – and within that adapt – a whole range of actions, motions and emotions.

On the inside, visualization is widely used as a creative and re-creative mental facility for how we react to changes in our reality.

The Experiment

I've always had a fascination with running experiments with some of the players I coach – with throwing balls at targets with eyes shut being the most memorable!

Recently I've been exploring the possibility of a player being able to mentally step out of what they are doing to become a 'virtual observer' of their own action – whilst at the same time performing that action. Although it is still relying on a lot of the Visual elements, I had an idea that something else useful would come along – not for everyone, but perhaps for certain players.

Whilst working with batsmen in cricket, I've invited them to find out whether they could project into an imaginary fielder standing close enough to be able to observe them as they bat. We used a bowling machine so that the ball delivered was consistent with one particular stroke in response. The players – already accomplished batsmen - were asked to play at between 6 to 10 balls received.

The range of reactions and their various abilities to "do the projecting" was as varied as I had expected. At one end of the scale the player said he couldn't do it at all, or so he felt. (Incidentally, this lad finds visualization difficult and displayed the same characteristics in the "Eyes Shut Throwing" experiment some 3 years earlier!) At the other end of the scale, the player reported the following:-

"Not sure I did the watching bit very well, but I did notice a feeling that I seemed to be very tentative in what I was doing."

Now it could be said that he was tentative because part of his attention was detached from concentrating on the ball. The thing is - in my view he didn't look tentative! It was **his own perceived** conclusion.

However, what happened for him when we went back to him just playing normally - allowing full attention to be brought upon the approaching ball – was noticeably different.

Before the experiment he had been playing well – after the experiment AND his own INNER FEEDBACK, he played with much more authority and in a much more positive way. I hadn't asked him to be less tentative and play in a more positive, assertive way. **Tentative** was his own description of what he felt he looked like – which made his inner adjusting process so immediate, ongoing and 100% effective. "Hard wired" is probably another way of describing it.

Given these criteria, could he have got this feedback any other way?
• This was a real-time experiment in Perceptual Positions and the response was also in real-time.
• The sensual information fed back was non-visual.
• It was his own information.
• Could a virtual simulator provide him with his own '2nd position' observation?
• Could video provide the Kinaesthetic data as feedback

Conclusion

This clearly works best with players with very good visualization and projection abilities. When it works, it works at lightning speed, and with immediate effect. By using the player's inner resources, any cross-sense translation is their own - such as his virtually-observed **V**isual to an inner-**K**inaesthetic. With this nothing is clouded by any coach's interpretation or linguistic capabilities - nothing is 'lost in translation'. It could almost be described as 'Clean Transformation'.

The experiment is an ongoing 'Work in Progress'.

The Session Built on Magic

One particular lad I coach (aged 14) is developing mental perspectives well outside 'the box' and part of the weekly challenge recently has been to explore differing mindsets and how the mind-body link with each one, plays out within the confines of his technique.

Choosing our Realities

This particular session I talked a lot about perspectives and realities – and how we make up our realities based upon our beliefs and experiences, and how these beliefs start out and grow. If we believe particular things about certain venues, certain opponents, certain playing conditions, certain arbiters and officials, certain selectors or examiners, certain coaches (and so on) then every one of the above "certain" scenarios is likely to have a negative or a constraining bearing (or effect) upon the way WE are going to play or perform – if we choose to let them do so.

Being at "Effect" rather than "at Cause"

The thing about all our different realities is this – each

one is just one version of "the truth" – His, mine, theirs etc. The thing is that no particular one is right, no particular one is more real in the real world than the other, and of course we can choose a different one every time.

However, taking this choice means we have come to a fork in the road, a fork where one way leads to being "at cause" and the other to being "at effect". To do this we adopt a particular mindset, in order to align our view of the world with our view of the physical and mental approach and behaviour we are going to take.

The choice is ALL ours - except that the choice of "at effect" doesn't actually feel like it is a choice **we** have made. The causes are all external, and we are the victims.
We're all familiar with limited beliefs and excuses such as these ...

* "But HE made me do it!"
* "I was distracted – they put me off my concentration"
* "The Ref was a complete idiot"
* "I didn't believe I was good enough"
* "Nothing felt right today"
* "My head was in another place"

* "We always lose to them – they're our bogey team"
* "I hate xxxx – he winds me up just being there" and so on.

These are all external or internal distractions that we have chosen to react to in a non-useful way.

Manipulating Realities and Framing Success

"So, do you enjoy magic – do you like watching magicians doing tricks?" I asked him. I noticed a half smile that said he knew some shift in perspective was just around the corner – and he nodded so I continued.

"Magicians have mindsets that are centred on trapping and focussing your attention on one thing and then changing the reality where you aren't paying attention. They also have, built into that mindset, a belief that they will always succeed."

He was showing attentive curiosity now...

"So in order for you to 'play magically' there is a mindset you can adopt that is very much like that of the magician."

The Magician's Mindset

"Most of us go into any contest, performance, action even, with what I call two frames of mind. There's the one based around what we want or would like to have happen – and there's the other based on what we don't want or hope won't happen."

This is akin to the famous phrase that says 'Those who believe they can and those who believe they can't, end up being both right' – because their actions are geared towards proving their beliefs.

"All the things that happen in the contest, performance, action, we then set about comparing with our two frames of mind – and in this we justify 'how things are going'.

If it's not going well then we react badly and if it's going well then we might get complacent. It's that mere act of comparison that torpedoes our performance. However –

if we go into the same contest, performance, action, with only ONE frame of mind, the success frame, the magician's **I-can-trick-you** frame, then whatever is going to happen is 'driven by us' in advance AND, curiously, we tend not to make any in-play comparisons either, leaving them until the event is well over. It's about changing the thinking from I-hope-to or I'd-like-to in favour of I'm going to"

"The other thing about the magician's mindset," I continued, "is the first bit - about focussed attention.

This is all related to our manipulating our reality or, in other words, playing with and changing the balance of our sensual input. The magician will direct what we are looking at by talking to us in a certain way and inviting us to feel things in a certain place. It's very cunning, and it plays with the balance of our senses in a way that we can't consciously control.

However, we can control it when we are being the magician to ourselves!"

Taking single-minded action

I invited my young client to step outside of his comfort zone and take the challenge of trying something different – and approaching it with a magician's mindset, to be single-minded.

There was a period of adjustment, especially as I hadn't invited him to do something quite like this before. Then, once auditory sensual data and internal dialogue was turned right down, the changes really began to take place in terms of visual-kinaesthetic.

He found the challenge exhilarating, physically as well as mentally tiring, and with some super-quality outcomes. It was interesting how he described it as mentally tiring, because he was treading uncharted territory, and this was something akin to hacking a new pathway through a "neural" jungle. I did point out that it would never be quite this tiring again.

The Priceless Comment!

Later when his one-to-one with me was finished and we were both engaged in some general activity with the rest of the players in the group, I made some remark to one of the others about being able to know what an opponent was going to do even before he did it. It was then that this particular young player grinned and asked,

"Pete, is this whole session this morning built on Magic?"

It was quite the most perceptive question I've been asked for a long time.

Conclusion

This was a timely reminder that when we are working with clients, one of the pre-requisites for great interaction, learning, changes and understandings, is **rapport.**

And, for me, part of the magic of coaching is rapport and where clients then feel able to go with whatever changes they want to bring about. Although in this case

I was guiding a player to break new ground, essentially part of our rapport was his trust that the new ground would be useful, purposeful, worthwhile to him as a player – and indeed as a person. Building a ground-breaking session for him within a frame of magic and artifice, was also ground-breaking for me too.

In reflecting upon our session and his amusing yet insightful remark, I have discovered that there is a great deal more for me to explore with other future clients, in terms of the concept of adopting the Magician's Mindset.

Work in Progress

It is a simple enough phrase - "Work in Progress"...

And yet I've discovered that when using it particularly with young sportspeople, that it actually liberates them from any performance shortcomings where (more often than not) they would hang their heads, beat themselves up, and all the other attributes that go with our culture of instant success, instant gratification, instant...you name it!!

So what is the power behind these three words?

1. Well, have a look at the *presuppositions* when the player hears my response to their assessment of how they've played.

PL: *"It went X, I did Y, I didn't do Z, I forgot to do M and I made a mistake with N"*
PW: "Yes - and let's be realistic now. These parts of your game – it is work in progress."

What is it? It is work >

which presupposes they are putting some effort into the activity away from competition; Which means they are motivated and pro-active towards getting to grips with these parts of their game.

What's happening to the work? It's in progress >

which presupposes it's on the move from A to B and is improving, getting better; Which implies positive and purposeful outcomes are already taking place.

2. Liberating emotional possession of competition errors.

What is the work in progress?

IT is! (a very nice little impersonal IT!) >

which actually puts a space between (1) the errors and imperfections of the performance and (2) the player themselves, by introducing that neutral and unemotional wedge (3), IT (i.e. the work being done to improve those particular parts of their game).

3. No impatient time constraints.

There's no start or finish to "Work In Progress" either - just a plan, a programme and record of improvement, accelerated or organic. These are process goals related to levels of competency, for which the acquisition timescale has never been set.

Part of the difference between my approach to young players and say those of the non-coaching fraternity (i.e. just adult players etc) - is this very point of detaching the emotional effect of errors of performance from the players themselves.

When young players are bombarded with a continual chorus from their seniors of "You should do X" and "You mustn't do Y" and (perhaps the funniest of all) "Don't forget to remember to do Z" - heavens, how confusing is that - these remarks are miles away from my "Keep on with the Plan - because this is all Work In Progress."

When to ease the Cognitive Load

See ball – hit ball

In certain sports where the players are endeavouring to hit a ball or a target, there is a very general coaching instruction to *watch the ball* or *watch the target*. The coach may specify this further by changing the word *watch* to *focus*, however there can be no doubt as to what the player is being expected to do. It is an instruction I myself have repeated countless times to countless players.

And yet here, in the minds of all players from beginners to experts, there runs a heuristic to *ease the cognitive load*. It is part of what "gets in the way" of performance for all players.
They start out by watching the ball or the target, and they may be expert enough at giving it their full attention.
However, the primary burning question is "For how long?"
The answer I got once from a very perceptive player aged just eleven was,
"For as long as I could tell what the ball was doing."

It made total sense to her to do it that way every time. Digging a little deeper revealed that she gathered enough information to enable her to decide which way (direction) to play the ball and how to hit it. However, the crux of her answer was this:

She watched it only for as long as she <u>thought</u> she needed to.

And when she missed the ball, or mis-hit it, it was her thinking that was at fault, not her watching. To put it another way - it was her decision when to *ease the cognitive load* on watching and switch it elsewhere (probably to initiating and executing the shot) that was at fault. She, like so many of us, was running a heuristic, a little macro routine, which turned watching the ball into *an educated guess*. Her decision to go into *guess-mode* was what, for her, lowered the drawbridge from the Castle of Cognition to the wide open intuitive spaces beyond the moat.

My job, as her coach, then became one of highlighting what was happening so she could change her map and navigate the entire routine to achieve a more productive outcome – a cleaner hit.

One time, I was explaining this to a fellow coach, who was well schooled in the more 'conventional' approach.
"So, Pete - isn't this nothing more than getting her to change her thinking?" he asked.
"To a certain degree you could say that, but your language shows that your own thinking is taking you in the wrong direction," was my reply. He appeared momentarily confused, but continued:
"So what about those coaches who point towards positive thinking as a means to help instil confidence, for instance? Isn't that, too, all about changing our thinking?"
(He's a great believer in the argument that for as long as we just focus on the positive then all will be well.)
"What I would say is this," I said. "Every player watches the ball. Whether it is the eleven year old student player or the very best player in the world, they are <u>both</u> only ever going to watch the ball for as long as they think they need to. They will do that every time they hit the ball, or play a shot.
So I'm definitely not going to be changing their thinking in that area."
"Yes, but ..."
"Look, it is all about the type of Language conveying the data, the information, the meaning. Positive thinking is all about filtering the <u>Verbal</u> Language *content* of the thoughts, conveyed via slow and ponderous cognitive

processing. Watching the ball is a thought *process* about gathering data in <u>Sensory</u> Language – running much faster at an intuitive level. These are both types of "thinking" – but there is no comparison after that."

"Ah, I see."

"So in terms of ball watching, I don't need to get my eleven year old student to change her intuitive thinking. We can certainly improve the quality of her sensory acuity, of course. However, that has nothing to do with changing her thinking! She needs to maintain that particular thought process and *Understand* that in order hit the ball better, she needs to watch for longer. No more – no less! This will inhibit the firing of this particular Heuristic for much longer AND mitigate the downside effects this heuristic causes – i.e. *Forcing her into guessing what the ball is doing.*

Likewise, I don't need to coach the best player in the world about watching the ball because he *Understands* that when he misses the ball or mis-hits the ball it is because he hasn't watched it for long enough. That's part of the territory that comes with *being the best* in the world."

"So what if the ball takes a dodgy bounce, or is blown by the wind? I've seen players go and look at the pitch or ground, or

complain about the weather conditions. What about that?"
"They may look at the pitch to satisfy their curiosity as to what made them miss, or grumble about the wind - however, the pitch and the conditions are the same for all players.

So what kind of processing is going on in each of their Minds to make the difference? Looking at the pitch is visual sensory data gathering, whereas a whole load of slow and ponderous cognitive verbalising goes into the activity known as grumbling."

Aside from the secondary major process of perfecting the physical *form* of playing the shots, hitting the ball – how they deal with the primary major process is what marks out the novices from the experts; and it is not the watching *per se*, but the thinking behind it.

Novices and experts <u>always</u> run the default heuristic of *educated guesswork* once they think they can tell what the ball is doing.

The experts have navigated enough hitting of balls to realise that they need to watch for longer, and that delays the running of the heuristic.

In terms of "brain-power", the experts allocate more band-width to their watching process. They don't *ease the cognitive load* on the primary major process, they ease, or even shut down on the other processes. They *manage their mental resources* better, in comparison to a novice. Even the experts though, can still fall into that mental trap of thinking they know and in those moments they become novices once more - because they are relying upon a Thought and not an Understanding.

Remember R D Laing's quote:

*"If I don't know I don't know, I think I know.
If I don't know I know, I think I don't know."*

Task Manager

If you look in the background at what is going on with your computer you'll locate the *Task Manager*. It is like a report of what processes are running, and how much processing power is allocated to each task. There are often quite a lot of tasks - ranging from how the information is put on the screen so you can see it, to where that information is drawn from, and so on.

Our computer has a set amount of RAM resources available to run tasks at a particular optimal processor speed. If we are running a lot of screens and some 'meaty' tasks then the *Task Manager* has a lot more on his plate in terms of how he is allocating resources through time. Some of the computer's performance will degrade if it approaches the limit of its resources. It will run much more slowly.

Eventually we'll get fed up with this downturn in performance and we'll go and upgrade our computer to one with more resources. When we upgrade with more RAM and a higher processor speed, then the *Task Manager* can cope with a lot more – *ergo* there is now no degradation of performance. Things run much better – and we are happy!

Our upgraded computer can handle its *cognitive load* with ease. Then, of course, we'll start getting it to do more for us by running more sophisticated processes that increase the cognitive load ... and so the whole cycle goes on.

However, that's how it works in computer terms – so what about US and our amazing human brain, for we are a million miles away from being a computer! For this I need to go back to my eleven year old player.

When she Understands that she needs to watch for longer, her *Task Manager* will change the resource allocation and she'll get better at her watching – and her playing.
We call this *watching for longer* a part of "paying better attention", or "better focus", or "better concentration."

We can "road-test" her *being better at watching* by adding to her Tasks and seeing what happens. The best way to do this is to throw in some distraction.
If she is "put off" by the distraction then her *Task Manager* has allocated some resources to paying attention to the distraction and gathering information about it. This has moved some of the resources originally allocated to watching the ball over to the distraction – and the result is degradation of outcome quality.
In terms of see ball – hit ball she won't be able to see ball as well so she won't be able to hit ball as well, if at all.

Moving on, when she gets *good at* dealing with distractions, then her depth and longevity of concentration will go up dramatically. And when she gets really good at dealing with the biggest distraction of all – herself – then she'll achieve a good level of self-mastery. She will be more expert than novice!

Mind you, she will still be vulnerable even then, because - for all of us - our attention ebbs and flows, our level of awareness fluctuates over time and through every moment.

A Partridge in a Petrie

Growing a Culture

I've set out on a journey into the unknown.
Well, it isn't entirely THE unknown, because it is a Cricket Project and it's a Coaching Project - and I work, ply some of my trade, coaching within the game of cricket. So, I'm doing a number of familiar things *"wot I luv"*.

And, if you can find that in life, it's a good place to be.

Yet – journeys into the unknown, for lots of us, can be filled with trepidation. We are stepping out and engaging with the unfamiliar. However, when we are *familiar* with the unfamiliar, comfortable with new things, then we really get to notice all the amazing changes going on around us – changes we are helping to bring about.

The need to seed

The project is in my home town – where cricket has been a *cinderella* sport for quite some time. There are in excess of a thousand children being educated on our turf, and the local cricket club is – like all sports clubs around the country – in constant need of younger personnel, both for their playing numbers and strength, and for the longevity of the club itself.

There is a need to seed some new culture – so we are doing it by following a successful model. We work with the children, starting in *their* most common environment (school), and then bring – encourage – those keen to play more cricket, to the cricket environment at the club.

It's the same I do with all new clients. I pace them at their familiar 'view of the world' and then lead them to other 'views of the world'. It is a simple model for changing perceptions, and as we know, when we change perceptions we change the world.

Modelling mode

In our last session, I'd got the lads to work on a particular shot that involved footwork – in particular we were working on using footwork to come down the wicket towards the ball, rather than just standing in our stance at the crease waiting for the ball to arrive. I talked about how we can sometimes become *'prisoners of the crease'*, by electing to play all our shots from there. This, for a lot of the time we are batting, is OK, yet there are times when it can prove particularly awkward for us.

And this, in a way, is the same with life. If we believe the crease is our *safe* area, then we'll view stepping out of it, as stepping into the unknown. However, for us to play some of the 'curveballs of life' in the best possible way, then we'll need to come out of the crease and step down the wicket.

So – it's a Culture. It's a culture for our life as well as a culture for batting. And when we want to embrace a culture, it needs to be big enough to embrace. And for it to be big enough to do that, we have to seed it and grow it. I think you can get the picture!

Getting the Picture

There are two basic types of shot in cricket – straight bat shots, where the bat is vertical, and cross bat shots where the bat is horizontal. The shot we were working on is a straight bat shot.

One of the lads was struggling to hit the ball using a straight bat, so I ran a few little sub-routines that broke

down the technique for him. He got the hang of them in the micro-detail, but when it came to put the sub-routines together he still struggled with the 'bigger picture'.
I then asked him if he played any other *striking the ball* sports and he said he played tennis.

"In tennis," I said, *"you are used to hitting the ball with extended arms, plus rarely are you playing any shots equivalent to this particular one in cricket. There are some cricket shots with extended arms, and you'll be very good at those because your body is familiar with how you want it to be positioned."*

"Familiar is the key," I went on, *"and WHEN your body gets familiar with straight bat shots in cricket, loads of new possibilities start to come along. At the moment things don't feel so good because you are **modelling** a technique you are **familiar** with in tennis and **mapping** it onto a cricket shot where it doesn't work well."*

It's a bit like having one road map (of Britain, let's say) and then trying to use it elsewhere (travelling in France for instance.) The moment we realise that there are many more maps than just the one we've got, then our bodies will go and get a map of France, or wherever we are endeavouring to navigate around.

As I said afterwards to one of the club's adult players who had been assisting, the tennis-playing lad will very quickly grasp playing straight bat shots – and only as quickly as he puts aside his entire Map of Tennis, and starts to **grow his culture**, which I called his Map of Cricket. Some parts of the maps will be quite similar – but in order for him to grow his entire range of skills, he'll need a range of maps and not just one.

Get out of Jail Free

All change is learning, and all learning is change. And to embrace change, like that, we need to loosen the chains of the prisons we have made for ourselves. For batting in cricket that might be remaining in the crease, for tennis it will be something else, for the person looking to get fitter it might be the excuses they make not to exercise, for the person with weight issues it might be the Comfort Food Zone. The list is endless.

We are modelling and seeding our cultures from the moment we are born. It is how we learn and grow.

At some point in our lives we may become aware of the way we are modelling and growing the seeds of our cultures. This is when we become directors of our lives. We then start to become good at our A-game. Yet in order to be good at our game, we also need to be **game – bold** – willing to play our ***Get Out of Jail Free*** cards.

So, whilst I've never heard of anyone growing a partridge – or indeed and game bird - in a Petri dish, we CAN all grow pear trees from seed.

Culture Shock

Spooking the Impala

One of my more oft-repeated mantras is
"Always Expect the Unexpected".
It is, I believe, good advice and practice, for embedded in there is a number of purposeful presuppositions and implied embedded commands.

Consider the impala drinking at the water-hole, noticing the crocodiles gliding around thirty metres away in the water – but failing to notice the lions creeping up behind.

Interestingly, looking out for the unexpected can give us a wonderful understanding about the nature of **Unexpectedness** and **Randomness** – like that! The world is random anyway, so we become more "at one" in spontaneity terms with what's going on. "Always" is a command, by way of a *caveat*, since it is also in our nature to be drawn into distractions and moments of un-readiness where our absorbed attention to the **Randomness** of things is diluted.

I was at one of my After School Cricket Clubs this week, talking with the players, when this **'*lion*'** caught me unawares.
"Are you a professional coach?"
"Yes."
"Where do you go?"
"I go to lots of schools and also clubs."
"Do you coach professionals?"
"I have done. They are professionals now though they weren't professionals at the time I coached them. They were just a few years older than you are now."
"So why have you come to OUR school?"

Just for a moment I felt the jaws of the lion about to close, yet with the speedy reactions of a spooked impala, I leapt back and to the side. In the real-time context of the Club, the question and the players waiting for my reply, there was a moment of complete suspension. Time stood still – tumbleweed rolled through the empty streets blown on the whistling frontier breeze. And in that moment I recalled some of the other times I'd darted away from the "jaws of the lion", by responding with total authenticity.

"Because I want to give YOU ALL a chance to enjoy some cricket by playing, and to help you and show you how to get better at it, so you can enjoy it some more. Which is why we're all here today – isn't it?"

Shock, Shocking and After-Shock

In the face of such a leonine attack, for me – the Impala - it was not so much 'fight or flight' but rather duck, weave, and counter punch. So maybe I wasn't *being Impala* at all! Maybe it was more like "wise old bird".

However, there is a bit of a delayed shock for me, as I reflect in the comfort of my own mind.

For the questioning child to ask why I should choose to go to THEIR school, there has to be a deeply felt opinion by them about the nature and culture of THEIR school and their place in it. And that opinion contains elements of cynicism, sarcasm, criticism and more than a hint of apathy bordering on depressive despair.
It would easy to think:
"How on earth can my simple message of learning through the fun of playing cricket compete against such a raft of powerful AND growing beliefs in the mind of a 10 or 11 year old."
For one hour a week they encounter my message, and for the remainder of the time their growing beliefs are reinforced by all the other inside and outside messages that bombard them on a daily basis.

Conclusion

It would SO easy for me to throw in the towel, by pointing a finger at the apparent collective culture of the playground of this school and say "enough is enough."

However, I am "wise old bird" who has, I'm pleased to say, been lucky enough to have worked in some pretty tough and challenging schools – in pretty tough and challenging neighbourhoods. For me, also, I am grateful for what I have learned about the equal psychologies of perseverance and non-reaction and why certain people, at whatever age, do what they do.

So cricket – and its wonderful message – goes on regardless. The choice for those who don't like what it is doing for and to them is "Quit and Sit" – rather than "Stay and Play".

For when we play, we can forget where we are, who we think we are, and just be totally engaged in the fun and the activity.

So next week we start again with a clean sheet, a blank canvas. The struggle of their culture versus mine that took place at the water-hole this week is a thing of the past. We have each learned something through that struggle. I know and understand what I have learnt and will use it, going forward.

They may already see their world in a slightly different way as a result of the struggle – and it would be if that were to be so. For however desperate or hopeless any culture may seem to those caught or trapped in it – we need to be and remain aware that a culture, any culture, is only perpetuated by failing to engage with it.

Attention Awareness Focus and Concentration

I was watching an episode in Professor Brian Cox's latest series **Wonders of Life** and moved to the edge of my seat as he began to talk about the senses, sensual data, and in particular - OUR senses.

Fascinating as this section was, I was hoping he would make reference, in detail, to our Reticular Activating System (or RAS). This is our brain's perceptive filter, where we 'let in' the data we want and 'ignore' what we don't want or feel the need to retain. I say "let in" here with a pinch of salted licence because in fact it is already "in our heads" anyway! It's just that we don't begin to perceive it until the RAS has screened it for our conscious awareness.

Over the years I've worked, particularly with sportspersons, on the ability to concentrate and how the RAS can really help us bring a level of control to our manipulation of sensual input. And there's an interesting co-relation here also with a number of hypnotic phenomena - analgaesia, amnesia and hallucination in particular - where perceptual distortions are taking place.

My recent and ongoing work with players from my county's Ladies' Cricket squad (coupled with watching Brian Cox) has brought me back to some of the experimental practical work I've done over the years in applying elements of the amazing powers available to us from within the functions of the RAS.

Watch the ball!

The old adage of "watch the ball (target, opponent, etc)" is a very simple coaching instruction, and yet how often do we get given the FULL instruction - the necessary detail that will really help us? "Watch the ball" is only the start and yet we might believe that just following "watch the ball" will give us everything we need to know about the ball and how we might strike, chest, punch, catch or kick it.

There is more to watching than meets the eye! There is:-

- *HOW are we watching?*
- *For how LONG are we watching?*
- *What level of DISTRACTIONS are happening?*

and so on and so forth.

Ok you could say these are all things that come under the umbrella labelled **Concentration** - but then do we ever get to learn how to concentrate? Did any teacher in school ever show you how to concentrate? You knew what was meant by *pay attention,* and you knew in particular how to make teacher think you *were* paying attention! We all have our own particular definition of what concentration is and (rather like "watch the ball") these all lie somewhere on a sliding scale of quality.

How, and for how long are we watching?

I once sat a group of sixteen young district level cricketers in a circle, with a cricket ball in the middle. I gave them a couple of minutes to study the ball and then tell me as much as they could about that ball. I got back a whole range of answers from the very obvious - it's round and red - to the detailed. I then got them to each handle the ball in turn, with their eyes closed, and then tell me what more they'd discovered about the ball by describing what they could feel.

This was an information gathering exercise about the ball, the kind of information useful to a bowler. The better the bowler, the more useful the information is -

and the better the bowler, the better the speed and volume of information gathering. In this exercise the RAS was being directed at characteristics of one object, and to be fair to the sixteen young players, the feedback was all bits of raw data - because that's what I'd asked for. If we'd done the exercise again with another ball, this time I'd have asked for "what do you notice that's different?" And this time the RAS would have been filtering for differences.

Whether it is noticing sameness, differences or patterns; seeing familiar faces in a crowd, hearing our name spoken in the hubbub of a crowded room or noticing subtle nuances in the tastes of wines - our RAS here is very much 'working to order', doing our bidding. However, I digress, so let's return to the RAS with regards to visual matters.

The level of distractions

Reduce the level of distractions and the quality of the processing of visual data goes up sharply. One of the things you can do is to direct the RAS to not process other incoming sensual data, such as sound distractions

- draw your auditory attention inwards or even off. It can be done by allowing yourself to become more visually absorbed - rather like the group of sixteen players had been - and with practice you can allow that absorption to muffle and shut out external sounds.

However - the biggest distraction to the working order of the RAS is our own internal dialogue, the demands of which seem to drain away the processing power necessary for good sensual filtering. Think of what was happening to your sporting performance when there was 'mental baggage' around to clutter up your clarity of mind. Your concentration and focus was indistinct and fuzzy, your decision making slow, unclear and flawed, your levels of physicality and athleticism degraded quicker.

If there was a way to leave that mental baggage in the changing room, or back at home, then we'd all do it wouldn't we?

If you subject yourself to a lot of self-talk, or find yourself turning over a lot of thoughts in your mind - notice what happens to that when you are drinking and, particularly, eating. Does it rest and then come back?

I've noticed, both with clients and myself, that when the tongue is engaged then internal dialogue is diminished. There is an **ideomotor** response associated with internal dialogue and major tongue activity (like chewing gum for instance) inhibits it. The whole thing about over-active internal dialogue is this - it isn't just with us in a sporting context. It's with us throughout our daily lives, and for us to 'kick it into touch' in our sport we need to deal with it everywhere.

"How do I do that – it is part of who I am," you might say.

It isn't part of who you are, it's just a habit you've learnt and become familiar with - and there are many ways of dealing with it, starting with telling that inner voice to "shut up!"

Trying hard to concentrate

It is said that to concentrate for long periods of time - especially in a sporting context - is an extremely difficult thing to do.

"You should have uptime and downtime, *ergo* developing an ability to switch on and switch off would be a really useful skill to master."

It is well chronicled that distractions such as pauses, intervals and other breaks in play often lead to dramatic changes in concentration levels for players. In these instances we might all think that those players had lost the means of switching concentration back on.

And yet when we are absolutely and totally absorbed in something - something that requires our **concentration** (whatever that may be) - we can be in uptime for hours. We can be totally focussed in something to such an extent that time seems to stand still, and those faculties that seem to deplete so quickly when we're putting effort into concentrating, are as fresh at the end of our activity as they are at the beginning.

So, where the powers of concentration and mental fatigue are concerned, perhaps the answer is this - we merely need to allow ourselves to become totally absorbed in the play and in the action.

It is easy to see, on reflection of course, that this is just another way of saying

"Play in the Now".

Conclusion

So did Brian Cox talk about the RAS with regard to the human senses? Sadly no, although he did go in another direction that was equally interesting, engaging and absorbing. The key thing for me was that the connection was made with my own discoveries.

We often make conscious directions and tunings of our RAS, although often just when we are performing an act of concentration. And even then - rather like the length, breadth and depth of quality "watching the ball" - we need to be aware there are degrees of focussing we can apply to our RAS as well. Familiarity and practice are necessary to maintaining and honing ALL our skills - and that includes the ones that go to make up what we call concentration.

Resilience

Currently, the buzzword in sporting circles is **resilience**. Given a run of poor results or performances, at any given time teams need more of it, whilst some of the individuals within the team have gained a lot more of it, some who had lost theirs have got it back, and some can't seem to find theirs right now. Individual players too suffer the same ebb and flow. Everywhere we turn, we hear resilience mentioned.

Because we give it a label, like confidence and charisma, it is immediately more tangible. It is – like a commodity – valuable, tradable, marketable. I expect there are, as I write, people in the great wide coaching world away from sport already billing themselves as Resilience Coaches.

Resilience in performance is described as the ability to remain composed, confident and consistent in the face of errors. A resilient player is one who can let go of errors and return to the present moment.

Back in 2004, courtesy of the Saturday morning Sky TV show Soccer AM, the word *"**bouncebackability**"* was coined and it became a bit of a *cult* word with sports fans, pundits and players. It took a rather sterile phrase from sports psychology - *mental resilience in sport* - breathed life into it, injected it with **pzazz,** and gave this six-syllable, concatenated construction a *street cred* that almost raised it to being inducted into the linguistic hall of fame called The English Dictionary.

These days, many things to do with the mental side of sport are much more widely mentioned and discussed in the media. Gone is the mystery and we regularly encounter commentators, pundits and players extolling the benefits and virtues of athletes being grounded, of having clarity, of being resilient., of being in a Flow State or in The Zone.

However, as we travel down the players' spectrum from elite to grass roots we still encounter a lot of the stigma associated with anything tagged with the words *mental* or *psychology*. There is still an old-school type of unease and distrust attached to anything referred to as being in the **mind** rather than in the **body**.
And it probably goes to the deep-seated fear in our

society of being dubbed as a bit of a head case, slightly weird, unhinged, not quite all there, not entirely in control, dysfunctional, having a problem, of being unable to cope, of being ill in the mind, of being – for all intents and purposes – BROKEN.

Our culture, built as it is upon the perfect ideal, can just about put up with broken bodies – but broken minds? Perish the thought. Yet, statistically, we are told that 1 in 4 people in the UK will experience a mental health problem each year.

Bouncing Back

So how can we get to be resilient in our sport – or indeed in our lives?

Can we learn *bouncebackability*?

The simple answer, of course, is yes.

Why do I say of course? Well, everything starts somewhere and we are not born with an innate understanding of making mistakes and getting over them. We first gain an understanding about making errors and mistakes, of getting things wrong, from our familial culture.

Later, as we first go to school, we discover more about errors, corrections and how society and the others around us judge the making of mistakes.

This early influence lays a very crucial foundation for our ability to be resilient. And when we are growing up and constantly learning things, this ability is with us every waking moment, and pervades every single thing we do.

This underlines my belief that everything, every action, in our lives is a unique performance, and is borne out by this famous quote by Heraclitus of Ephesus:

"No man ever steps into the same river twice, for it's not the same river and he is not the same man."

You could say that we are all of us *at the mercy of* our early influences, so much so that by the time we are seven we have already been put on the road to becoming either a very resilient performer, a confidence player or a perfectionist, or somewhere in between!

However, although this might presuppose that we cannot get off that ROAD once we have been put on it, we are subject to influence and persuasion all the time. And it is the influences we encounter at any time that can steer us elsewhere and to enable us to perform in a different way, and perhaps a more successful or a more fulfilling way.

Gaining a Foothold on Resilience

Once we know there is another ROAD, that we are not doomed or BROKEN, and that there is such a thing called **resilience**, we can start to discover more about how we can make our performances more consistent and rewarding, and fuse our love of our sport with the joy and ecstasy of doing it to the very best of our abilities, in the moment.

Gloria Solomon and *Andrea Becker* (2004) came up with an interesting acronym that described a four step process they developed to help athletes deal with performance errors.

A.R.S.E

A =
Acknowledge the error and the frustration it has caused
R =
Review the play and determine how and why the error occurred
S =
Strategise a plan to make the necessary corrections for the future
E = Execute and prepare for the next play

Amusingly, they described this as *"teaching athletes this sequence will give them a tool for managing the emotional response which comes with making mistakes, and help them to get their ARSE in gear!"*

Arseing about

I am coaching an 8 year old at the moment who is very keen on his cricket and has above average talent. I noticed early on that if he perceived some part of our practice as being a *performance*, a *contest*, then his behaviour changed.

He would hit the ball, make a slight error, fall to the ground whilst saying in a miserable tone of voice how he'd got it wrong, messed it up, and seemed inconsolably upset with himself. He appeared to become a near perfectionist and probably had about 5% resilience.

Without consciously realising it at first, I ran the ARSE strategy and got him back on his feet and ready to play the next ball. I got him to hit 10 balls at a target in this little contest, and after every error he ran his sequence and I ran the ARSE strategy.

Now the interesting thing here was that not only was he learning how to be more resilient, but he was also learning about MY coaching culture, and my approach to helping people get over errors and to getting better. By the time we'd moved on to practicing another cricket skill, he'd grasped the whole idea of how we get better at something by making mistakes and getting it wrong.

Work in Progress

I've worked with enough perfectionists and confidence players over the years to know that it is definitely a player's *thinking* that gets them into a place of low resilience, and that it is definitely their thinking that is getting in the way of their performance.

The **Secret** – or this particular version of it – is to liberate them from the NEED to *Listen to their own Thinking*. We all have a tendency to hang onto the familiar, and the more familiar we are with Listening to our own Thinking then the more we will hang on to the NEED to do it.

I first used the phrase ***Work in Progress*** (see p 173) some years back, with a lad who was inhibited by perfectionism even in practice, let alone in performance. We would be working on some particular skill and his behaviour would change as a result of his (in his eyes) making a mistake – getting it wrong. In a way he resembled my recent 8 year old, in that he struggled with the emotional outpouring initiated by his **Inner Judge**.
After I explained to him about practice and progress –

like that - I watched him listening and nodding, and somewhere inside he made the connection and got his ARSE in gear!

Almost at once he stopped beating himself up in practice. Before the next match he was due to play, I talked with him about how we can take our *Work in Progress* into a contest. He made mistakes – and he dealt with them well. From that moment on he became a resilient player, and he understood resilience even though we never talked about it.

Conclusion

As a Performance Coach who also works as a technical coach, I consider myself lucky to be in a unique position to be able to embed and interweave one discipline within another. As a result I'm able to raise the resilience of grass roots players without having to tell them that we are going to work on some *mental* skills. Likewise I'm able to influence an eight year old in terms of resilience, knowing that that growing understanding will help him in other parts of his young life.

I was having a casual chat recently with some sporting folk and someone said,
"Everyone talks about resilience now. Is that like bouncebackability?" I nodded. *"Wish I had it."* He continued, *"Wish I could get some of that. Of course it's only for professionals and those at the very top of the game."*
"What makes you think that?" I asked, quite curious about his perspective.
"Well it wouldn't work on me would it? It's all to do with what's going on in here," he said, tapping the top of his head.

I leaned forward and looked straight at him,
"How do you know you haven't already got some resilience?"

Our Stance in Life

I started coaching cricket to two very young lads a few weeks ago. Now I may look old-fashioned but the time-worn phrase "In my day..." is not part of my coaching stock-in-trade.

I showed them both how to **stand** ready to receive the ball and one of them disagreed and said "This is how my Dad showed me to do it."
Suddenly, here we were – on a communications roundabout with many exits. Had I looked at the signposts before entering the roundabout? Did I really want to cite his Dad as being 'wrong' – did I really want to explode his belief that his Dad was his 'best' model in life? Maybe I was the first 'proper coach' he had ever encountered in his young life so far – so was I to **insist** that he follow my instructions?

Of course not! These are three exits I would want to avoid like the plague!

The thing is – if he'd encountered me ten years ago, I'd have shown him the way *I was taught*, which was probably the way his Dad was taught too:-

During the intervening years I saw – and tried out for myself – the stance I now advocate, especially for beginners.

There's a simplicity to it which is one of the reasons that it really works. There's also a logic to it that facilitates a number of other things that really do need to be correct for the next stage to work well. It's a gateway that works when it is open, but that when shut you might vault the gate and fall flat on your face in a cow-pat!

Our Stance in Life

There's a parallel with our batting stance in cricket and our stance in Life. And it's a parallel that actually matches these two young lads also.

Ten years ago I **could** have chosen to stay with the way I'd stood to bat all my life. The tried and tested, *this works for me because almost everyone stands this way* method; the *its always served me well except when it hasn't* method; the *I'm too old to try something new* method; the *this is the way my Dad* taught me* method. (* And Dad here is a euphemism for society, peers, mates, the world, our culture, as well as dear old Dad himself.)

But I didn't.

I tried it out to see what was different, what felt different, how it changed the way I played, whether I felt happier with it, whether it brought me success, whether it **worked** – ALL purely from my own perspective. Once I had the answers and installed it as an unconscious competence in terms of an applied skill – then I knew I would never change back. PLUS, as a coach I could now be utterly authentic in the way I was passing on the skill to others.

We all have some things we'd like to change in our lives – things we are doing, ways we are doing, that we would prefer having better results, better outcomes, more success from. It could be about certain habits or behaviours – like smoking, our relationship with food, our relationships with others, our relationship with ourselves, our fears, our worries and anxieties, and so on.

These things are all part of our lives until we change them. They are all part of our stance in Life. Now, if we want to see whether how we are batting in life might be improved by changing our stance – what could be simpler than just *giving it a go*?
"Pete, you make it sound so easy, but I can't seem to do it."
"Ah – I said it was **simple**, I didn't say it was **easy**."

"The process is what's **simple**. The **ease** with which you do it is entirely up to you.
You can make it easy – like I did when I changed my stance – by just accepting all that the process entailed,

and noticing what was different every step of the way. Or you can make it complicated and difficult - by noticing the difference as discomfort; noticing what your peers, friends, colleagues think and believe (what your Dad says); by telling yourself it can't work, it isn't working, it won't work, it'll never work.
The choice – as always – is yours."

The Lads

So the lads tried my invitation to stand *this* way and hold the bat like *that* – they gave it a go! You could say they politely indulged my suggestions! And, lo and behold - as if by magic – they found that hitting the ball really well, and so much better and more consistently than before, was starting to come much, much easier to them. Their eyes lit up, they beamed with smiles of self-fulfilment and, although I don't know for sure, probably went home and said to Dad, "This is the way to bat. You try it!"

Learning from Mr. Li

Many years ago, when I was a student in Accountancy, I went on a month-long revision course to give me the boost to get over the intermediate qualifying line in my chosen profession. It was, for me, something of a last chance saloon - "Pass and move on; Fail and you cannot take this exam again." Passing was my only ticket to becoming a fully-fledged Accountant.

There were around sixty of us on this classroom-based course, representing a cross-section of working students in our field. Some worked in London, in the City, for the well-known firms; others from further afield, but still in big practices in the provinces. I was a rarity – for I came from a very small firm out in the sticks. While others worked mostly in big audit teams, I worked alone on accounts of small businesses, with incomplete records. I did my fledgling accountancy work from the start to the finished article – which I then handed over to one of the partners for them to liaise with the client.

The course was run by two Indian gentlemen who were as different as chalk and cheese. One was a wise old bird, nearing retirement and who talked with a very thick accent. He was the course principal. The other was in his late twenties, spoke with an Oxford accent and had passed his Accountancy Finals with honours as a national winner for his year. Their teaching styles were also *chalk and cheese* – and most of us realised after the first day that the principal would ask a question and choose someone from the sea of hands that went up, whilst the young tutor had the names of all the students always to hand. He would ask the question and then say who he wanted to answer.

These differing class-tutoring styles elicited equally different levels of concentrated engagement from Us. With the young guy's questioning style, we ALL had to have an answer ready – whereas with the principal, if we weren't keen to answer then we just didn't put our hands up.

We had a fellow student of oriental extraction – called Mr. Li. We never knew his first name. Mr. Li liked questions because, it seemed to the rest of us, he knew all the answers. No matter which tutor's class it was, his hand went up at every question asked. And if the tutor paused, to either pick or say a student's name, Mr. Li would wave his hand vigorously, begging attention. **"Me, sir, me sir! Please pick me!"** he seemed to say. Needless to say to the rest of us – long since out of school – this was more than a shade comical. Yet we were polite young professionals, so Mr. Li's classroom demeanour continued unchecked right across the four weeks of the course.

After the two examination days, we all met up in class for our final get together with each other and the tutors. There was light hearted conversation and plenty of banter throughout the room, and then our tutors wished us well.

Just before we dispersed and went our separate ways, one of our fellow students went to the front. He thanked the tutors on our behalf and then announced a special award for the student who had made the biggest impression upon the rest of us. It was a bit like a "mini-Oscar's".

He mentioned a couple of his city colleagues as nominees and then announced the winner –
it was Mr. Li.

We all laughed, shouted and cheered as Mr. Li went up to collect his award … a Wooden Spoon.

Wherever we go, 'e goes with us

One of the dangers in all learning is to assume that we have arrived. Or in other words, that we know it all and there is nothing more to learn. Believing *"I can do it now,"* is one of those times when life bites us in the butt.

A young lad came to his first cricket club session with us and I admired his considerable, yet raw, talent as a bowler. It was his first encounter with my coaching style, and I gave him some technical advice which he applied well, and we both saw an improvement in the outcomes of every ball he bowled.

After about fifteen minutes I spoke to him with a high degree of praise, for I really was well impressed.
I wanted to make an impression on him – as he had done on me.
The next ball he bowled was so wide it hit the side of the nets and never even reached the batsman.
"Oh No!" I called out as I went to give him the ball back. *"I shouldn't have said all those things I've just said!"*

We both laughed and he went back and carried on bowling impressively.

Part of my lifelong learning as a coach is that I have seen this happen so often and with players of all ages. I knew that the praise would be a distraction; and the distraction plays out because of the EGO.

The EGO, his ego was awakened by my praise and, all of a sudden, his mental state as he went back to bowl the next ball was more focussed on my words than the next piece of action. In the lapse of time between hearing my words and letting go of the next ball he bowled, his ego was saying to himself "**I can do it now – I know it all – There is nothing more to learn.**"
In reality he had discovered the complete opposite.

Now my little ruse, the trick I'd played, had worked a treat for him.
Why?
Because he had both laughed at himself and then returned 100% to bowling as well as he had done before the praise. In that moment, he had conquered his Ego. If he had not laughed, let's say, then Ego would have held sway, and would have continued to distract the rest of his action.

And I see this all the time too. We utter words of disappointment, we breathe deep sighs, we get cross with ourselves, we beat ourselves up verbally, we blame it on something or someone. These are all examples of Ego holding sway. Keeping us from what we should REALLY be doing.

Conclusion

So, what are the parallels here between my young cricketer and Mr. Li?

Mr. Li is Ego by another name.
So, in order for you to get the point here, you need to forget the real person in Mr. Li.

All that the character Mr. Li wanted to do was to let the tutors AND everyone else know that he knew the answer AND it was imperative that he was recognised as knowing so. His hand waved at every question – *"Me, Me – Ask Me for I Know!"*

Of course, Mr. Li's only true reward was the *Wooden Spoon*. And thus it is, also with us, as we play out the various actions in our lives, whether at our sport, our work, our social interactions, our relationships, and with our selves. We have the propensity to garner a lot of wooden spoons.

As Ryan Holiday says in his book, *"Ego is the Enemy,"* when our attention is distracted –

"Do I _need_ this? Or is it really about ego? Am I ready to make the right decision? Or do the prizes (the praises) still glitter off in the distance?
To BE or to DO – Life is a constant roll call."

Footnotes

"Any active sportsman has to be very focused; you've got to be in the right frame of mind. If your energy is diverted in various directions, you do not achieve the results. I need to know when to switch on and switch off: and the rest of the things happen around that. Cricket is in the foreground, the rest is in the background." ~ Sachin Tendulkar

"Cricket was my reason for living - Down the mine I dreamed of cricket; I bowled imaginary balls in the dark; I sent the stumps spinning and heard them rattling in the tunnels." ~ Harold Larwood

"To me, it doesn't matter how good you are. Sport is all about playing and competing. Whatever you do in cricket and in sport, enjoy it, be positive and try to win." ~ Sir Ian Botham

"To me, cricket is a simple game. Keep it simple and just go out and play." ~ Shane Warne

Recommended Reading

The Practicing Mind:
Developing focus and discipline in your life
~ By Thomas M Sterner

The Inside – Out Revolution
~ By Michael Neill

The Open Focus Brain –
Harnessing the power of Attention to heal mind and body
~ By Les Fehmi PhD and Jim Robbins

Mapping the Mind
~ By Rita Carter

Clean Language:
Revealing Metaphors and Opening Minds
~ By Wendy Sullivan and Judy Rees

About the Author

Peter Wright talks about his life's pathways:-

Everything has a purpose, and my long and varied working life has enriched this purpose with experience; from accounting, financial control and developing IT systems in small companies – to working as a self-employed chef and hotelier, and specialist record retailer.

Add to that mix full time grounds-man at my local cricket club for several seasons, playing guitar and performing solo, duo and in small combos to mainly medium sized audiences over a number of years, and being active in a variety of sports both on and off the field and you can understand why I have such a burning passion for sport, music, performance and creativity!

In the early 1990's I starting coaching sport in earnest and very soon began taking a passionate interest in practical sports psychology – starting with my own game. The changes were astonishing, and I realised that legendary baseball coach Yogi Berra was right when he said, "90% of this game (or any game) is half mental."

In 2005 I gave up "the desk job" to become a full-time professional coach (specialising in cricket and rugby), and expanded this into mainstream therapy and performance coaching, using Hypnotic Phenomena, NLP and TimeLine™ Therapy, Clean Language, TFT, IEMT amongst a wide range of techniques and methodologies.

This is now a large part of what I do – coaching and mentoring from a mental perspective, helping people enhance what they do from the inside > out. From learning new skills or correcting old habits, to bringing a mental resilience to their performance, I'm there to enable them to enhance the quality of their lives.

And therein lies my constant goal with everyone I work alongside, regardless of age - to make a difference for them in whatever context they might want to make changes in their lives, going forward.

Peter writes regular articles on his blog at http://pjwhypno.blogspot.co.uk/

You can follow Peter online on Twitter @GourouxPete and @HaveMind2 and also on Facebook as Peter Wright.

Other books by Peter Wright:

Don't think of a Black Cat
A Beginner's Guide to NLP

Mind How You Go
Steps to enhance your life's journey

Lamplighters
Keeping the metaphorical streets of our life well lit

Mind How You Play
Enhancing your Sporting Performance
from the Inner Perspective

Gateways to The Zone
Pathways to Peak Performance

Navigating the Ship of You
Part 1 - A Guide through Thought and Language
Part 2 – Some Chronicles of a Navigator

The Cactus Approach
Building Blocks for Invincible Teams

Printed in Great Britain
by Amazon